DINING WITH ELEPHANTS

by

Françoise Malby Anthony

Managing director and co-founder of
Thula Thula Private Game Reserve, Zululand, South Africa

Author of two international bestsellers
An Elephant in My Kitchen (2018)
The Elephants of Thula Thula (2022)

First published in 2025 by Rockhopper Books
Unit A Victory Park, Capricorn Business Park, Muizenberg, 7945

Text © 2025 Françoise Malby-Anthony

Book cover, food, and staff photos by Christopher Laurenz and Isabel Marques

Wildlife photos by Thula Thula Game Reserve

Illustrations of elephants by Aimee Coyne

Cover design by Gouri Barua, Ruby Oldroyd

Layout and design by Gouri Barua

Edited by Michelle Meyer

Proofread by Anneke Labuschagne

ISBN 978-1-0492-0181-8

THULA THULA

RECIPES

This book is a celebration

This is more than a cookbook. It is a love story – to food, to the wild, and to the magic that happens when we choose to live alongside nature. It is about co-existence, sharing space with wild wisdom and discovering humility in the presence of true intelligence.

Over 27 years of living deep in the African bush, this book is a collection of true stories – hilarious, heart-stopping, and deeply human.

It is a testament to the power of dreams and that passion, vision, and perseverance can lead us to our wildest goals. It has been, and continues to be, a journey of discovery and survival for all of us, humans and animals alike.

But above all, it is a love letter – to the animals who welcomed us, to the land that held us, and to the incredible people who made it all possible.

Nana, our legendary matriarch

When French cuisine meets the wilds of Zululand

This story is a feast of close encounters. Cheetahs hunting at your front door, baboons in the swimming pool, and a bush baby at the bar. Then there are elephants strolling past your table, rhinos deciding to redecorate your lodge veranda, and the monkey mafia making off with the croissants.

Over the years, this place became more than a lodge. It became a living, breathing example of how hospitality, conservation, and culinary passion can intertwine. Every meal served was a tribute to the land.

This book is your invitation into a world where the wild teaches us everything we forgot to remember, with the unspoken wisdom animals carry with them – if we're humble enough to listen. Because we live with nature, not on top of it.

This cookbook is a celebration of that journey. Of the elephants. Of the wild. Of the food. Of the women who grew into brilliant chefs, and the stories we will share across generations and cultures.

Food. Fun. Wild.

I wanted this cookbook to be entertaining, educational, and just a little different.

Creating dishes in the middle of nowhere, with limited supplies, was definitely going to provide mental stimulation, a way to express my endless imagination.

Not always to the desired results, though. You cannot always win, and my wild creativity occasionally led to spectacular culinary disasters…

We opened the *Elephant Safari Lodge* in June 2000 and the Luxury Tented Camp in 2006. I started employing and training young Zulu women from nearby rural communities. Needless to say, communication was often quite challenging.

The Zulu women were very eager to learn, even from someone who came from a country where eating snails and frogs was part of her culture…

Trying to cook French cuisine in the middle of the bush with the closest supermarket 25km away was going to be an experience.

I was ready for this new adventure.

The elephants of Thula Thula

The beginning of a wild adventure

Lawrence, my late husband, and I decided to move into a small, run-down game reserve in Zululand in 1998. I was a complete city girl with no idea what I was getting into. I had lived in Durban for 10 years after leaving Paris, and I was just starting to adjust to living in a small provincial town. I suddenly landed in this new world, totally unprepared for a life in the middle of nowhere, among wild animals.

In those days, it was just a couple of impalas, nyalas, and giraffes. That was all. Until we received a desperate phone call from an elephant welfare organisation proposing that we take up the challenge of rehoming a herd of seven elephants.

They were labelled as 'rogue' and 'problem elephants'. When asked if we were willing to welcome them at Thula Thula, we just said yes, without asking too many questions, not imagining that this decision was going to change our lives forever.

The herd of seven arrived after a gruelling 16-hour journey in August 1999. They were placed in the boma, a one-hectare enclosure where they were meant to acclimatise to their new home, new environment, and new humans.

Only 24 hours later, we discovered exactly why they were considered 'problem elephants'. They broke out. Expert escape artists, they vanished into the wild.

The rest is history.

The herd of seven on their arrival in August 1999

What followed was an extraordinary journey of survival, trust, and transformation – not only for the elephants, but for us too. Their story has since been shared in three international bestsellers, touching hearts around the world and turning these once-feared elephants into beloved ambassadors for their species.

Since my arrival in 1998, life here has been anything but predictable. Expect tales of wild animals invading my garden, our safari lodge, and any other place we humans thought belonged to us… or perhaps it was always theirs?

Welcome to Thula Thula. Where the wild ones rule and teach us how to truly live.

" People with great passion can make the impossible happen. "

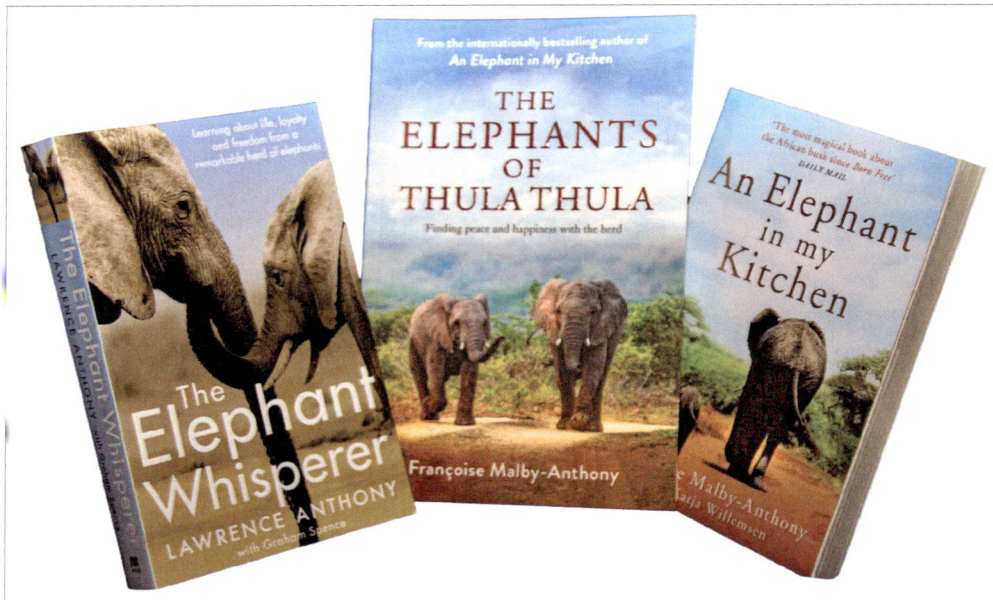

The story of Thula Thula

Welcome to life in the wilds of Thula Thula

My special and numerous rescued pets are always a great inspiration for me, as they are part of the testing and tasting team. So valuable when you like to experiment…

They witnessed my first days at Thula Thula in 1998. I had two Staffordshire Bull Terriers, Max and Tess, and my famous Bijou, a miniature Poodle, the Queen of Thula Thula.

Let's just say things are never boring when you share your life with a pack of rescued characters.

The main house was a run-down farmhouse, and the kitchen had a broken aircon that hung precariously above the stove. I was cooking rice in this very old kitchen when, suddenly, I saw a tiny mouse falling off the broken aircon.

To my horror, a snake followed. Both fell onto my stove.

Watching a snake swallow a mouse was something I never imagined experiencing. I had never met a snake before, and went into panic mode. So did my dogs. The entire kitchen turned into a zoo on fire. All of us bolted out of the kitchen, screaming, barking and all, and called the security guard on duty to help.

Now, Zulus living in rural areas are terrified of snakes, and they killed the invader without hesitation. We had no idea about snake identification. Only later did we realise that it was a totally harmless bush snake.

That was then. Today, things are very different at Thula Thula.

No creature – no matter how small, slithery, or suspicious – is killed here. Not a mouse, not a spider, and certainly not a snake. Over the years, I've learnt that every creature has a role to play. Whether it flies, crawls, gallops, or hisses, it belongs, just like we do.

Cohabitation isn't always easy, but it's essential. After all, we're all tenants on the same planet. And that, in a nutshell, is what we teach at Thula Thula: Education is the heartbeat of conservation.

The more we understand, the more we protect. And sometimes, learning starts with a snake falling out of your aircon.

Cooking with my fan club

> The secret to survival is the ability to adapt to a new situation.
>
> Change is inevitable, and pressure, challenges, and obstacles are a necessity for evolution and growth.
>
> It is the way we respond to it which makes the difference, and makes us realise that sometimes the impossible is achievable.

Seven elephants in my garden

It all began 26 years ago with the original herd of seven. Just after their release from the boma enclosure, they wandered into our unfenced garden. It was a surreal sight.

Frankie, one of the older females, was in the middle of the garden, mischievously chasing one of my kittens, while Nana, our legendary matriarch, made a slow and deliberate approach towards the house.

I'll never forget that moment, standing on the veranda, only a metre away from this towering giant, feeling smaller than ever. Nana looked straight at us, Lawrence and me, calmly, curiously. She could have easily pushed her way inside had she wanted to. Her presence was immense, four tonnes of quiet power and intelligence. Standing right beside her was her young son, Mandla, just two years old, eyes wide and eager. Perhaps he, too, was curious about what lay beyond the door.

My dogs, constant companions and beloved members of my life, had always found survival in the wild relatively easy, thanks to my overprotective instincts. But I knew elephants are not fond of noisy dogs. In a mild panic, I ran to our room and tried to hide them in the wardrobe. In my frantic state, I didn't notice that the other door of the wardrobe was open. So, as I tossed each dog inside, they kept popping out the other side, utterly confused, perhaps thinking it was some new game I had invented.

Back on the veranda, Lawrence spoke gently to Nana, soothing her with calm, reassuring words. She slowly backed away. The rest of the herd followed, leaving the garden as quietly as they had entered, disappearing into the bush.

But the image that stayed with me was little Mandla – the baby of the herd – running to catch up with his mother, always shielded by the others. Even then, he was a gentle soul, just like his mum Nana. Today, he is 28 years old, a magnificent bull and the largest elephant on our reserve.

When the herd comes to visit us now, we watch them from the pool area, filled with awe. And when Mandla walks past, he always gives a subtle nod, almost a bow, as if to say, "Hello. Remember me? I also wanted to come inside your house."

I once had the most beautiful fruit and vegetable garden

This garden was created with love by a gardener whom I called Papa John. He was a frail old man who took pride in his job. Every single lettuce, tomato, courgette, spinach leaf butternut, mango tree, and pawpaw tree was planted in perfect order. Created with love.

Our herb garden, too. Every herb you can imagine, much needed in the French cuisine we were creating at the lodge with fresh organic products, was present.

Watching the tomatoes and lettuce reach their harvesting time was an immense pleasure for Papa John.

It was a chef's dream, a gardener's triumph… and an elephant's buffet. All they left were the lemons and the chillies. Papa John was devastated, just like his garden. But we did not give up. We started again, and recreated a magnificent display of organic fruits, vegetables, and herbs. However, it was exactly the same scenario – as we were ready to reap the harvest of our hard work, the herd got in first and devoured it all.

We could not remain angry, though. Nana was just doing her job of leading her family to the best food. And with elephants being fussy eaters, Papa John and I took it as a compliment to have these returning guests showing such appreciation for the array of delicacies we had created.

Always looking on the positive side in life…

The lesson learnt from this experience is that elephants do not like acidic tastes and hot spices. For the security and safety of our wildlife, we installed numerous infrared surveillance cameras all around the game reserve.

Most of them were set up in trees with direct views on the fences, to deter intruders, and around the waterholes, where poachers liked to place their cruel snares to catch wildlife.

But our cameras kept being destroyed, found smashed down below the tree or just disappeared. Our poor security team was baffled, and convinced poachers were destroying them... until we received a photo from one of the cameras.

A close-up. Of a trunk. The world's first elephant selfie. Mystery solved; culprit found.

Elephants did not like any strange items put into THEIR trees.

Our dear pachyderms could not understand that the cameras were placed for their protection as well as our other precious wildlife. So, they just decided to grab them and put them down.

The solution: we smeared a generous mixture of lemon and chilli paste around each camera. We never lost a camera again.

Baby elephant rescue

It is not every day you find a baby elephant in your garden. But one unforgettable evening, that is exactly what happened.

Tom, my chef at the safari lodge, came knocking on my door with wide, wild eyes. "There's a baby elephant in the garden!" he blurted out.

I thought I must still be dreaming. It sounded completely surreal.

But there she was. Just seven days old, about 120kg of soft, lost innocence, standing unsure under the trees. We slowly coaxed her inside the house, and soon she was standing in my kitchen. With the help of Tom and a dedicated carer, we prepared a warm mixture of milk and water, following the vet's advice. She drank hungrily, then, like any baby after a good meal, curled up and had a nap… in my lounge.

While she slept, our game rangers combed the reserve in search of her mother. How she became separated from the herd – and why the herd had not come back for her – remains a mystery. Elephants are known for their deep family bonds, and questions like these may never be answered.

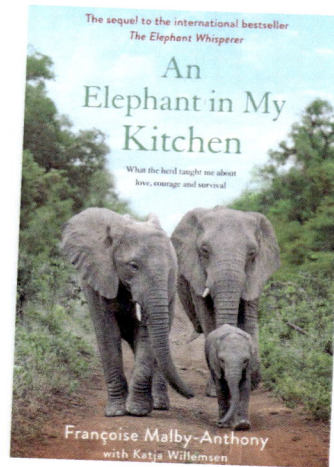

The sequel to the international bestseller
The Elephant Whisperer

An Elephant in My Kitchen

What the herd taught me about
love, courage and survival

Françoise Malby-Anthony
with Katja Willemsen

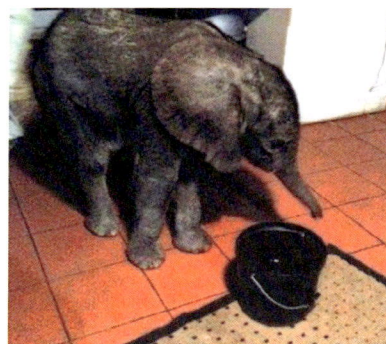

A few hours later, after much searching, her family was found. We gently lifted her into the back of a bakkie, with Tom riding alongside her like a proud guardian, and drove her back to her mother. The moment she saw her mum, she ran straight to her – and never left her side again.

It was an incredible and emotional rescue – one made possible thanks to the quick action of Tom, who noticed the little elephant wandering alone in our garden.

We named her Tom, in honour of her unlikely hero. Today, she is a beautiful teenager, still happily living here at Thula Thula – and still, in a way, part of the family.

An *Elephant in My Kitchen* was my first book, from that lost baby who inspired me to write her story, but also all the many wild adventures of Thula Thula, talking about my arrival in South Africa in 1987, and all that followed with our move to the wilds of Zululand in 1998.

The book also marked a turning point in my life. It was my way of showing the world that Thula Thula lived on, even after Lawrence – my husband, the Elephant Whisperer himself – passed away in 2012. Losing him was a shock that left me reeling. Suddenly, I was alone, facing enormous responsibility, grief, and a future I hadn't imagined navigating solo.

The book was released in 2018 in the UK and all English-speaking countries and was a huge success. I promoted it on social media as the follow-up to the international bestseller *The Elephant Whisperer*, written by Lawrence in 2009. The title I had chosen was fun, but reality as well. I really had a baby elephant in my kitchen.

One day, on a well-known social media platform, I saw the most incongruous comment from a lady who wrote: "How can you cook an elephant?" A bit confused at first, I took it as a joke, and I responded: "Easy! You just need a very big pot and voilà!"

My response was not to her taste as she replied with a series of insults that I chose to ignore. Responses arrived from all around the planet from Thula Thula fans, those who had read the book.

The situation was so absurd. This keyboard warrior who attacked me was shut up very fast by all our fans and disappeared from my page.

Thula Thula's reputation as elephant eaters was saved!

Hopefully, *Dining with Elephants* will not create such confusion...

An elephant in my garden

Frankie was a different story. You cannot tell a four-tonne elephant to stop walking into your garden. She was our fierce and highly respected matriarch, quite unpredictable at times. She was a different kind of matriarch from our gentle and wise Nana, helping to lead the herd as Nana's eyesight was fading.

That day, by stepping into my garden, despite the electric wires on the ground at the entrance, which was quite brave, I think she was just trying to get my attention, and maybe tell me something.

Frankie and I had a special relationship. We shared the same name – Frankie was my nickname as nobody could pronounce my very French name, Françoise. Lawrence decided to give her that name because, according to him, we had the same 'temperamental character'.

Whatever he meant by that.

So there she was, striding confidently through the garden like she was inspecting a property she might buy, while I watched from the bedroom window – me frozen in place, my dogs shivering at my feet.

We didn't know it then, but a few months later, we discovered Frankie was ill. And like the noble soul she was, she left the herd. She didn't want to slow them down, didn't want to be a burden. So she wandered alone, her independence intact, her pride still fierce.

This book is all about food, so it feels right to mention the special meals we prepared for her. My game ranger, Andrew, and I would bring her nutritious treats – meals with purpose – wherever she was in the reserve. Gourmet room service, bush style.

Elephants are usually great eaters, but we could see her appetite fading with her strength. Still, Frankie remained regal until the very end. Even in sickness, she walked tall. Literally – through my garden, my fears, and right into my heart.

Frankie coming in and out of my garden

As we mentioned in the fruit and vegetable garden episode, elephants are fussy eaters, so we had to prepare the best for her.

She had lost a lot of weight. So only cabbage, apples, and oranges, which were her favourites. All in a huge bowl that we dropped in front of her, calling her to get her lunch, as we do with our pets. I must say it was quite fun to watch her digging into her huge bowl and throwing away with her trunk the bits she did not like. As if she was saying, "Don't give me this again". That was our Frankie, that we all loved and respected for her strength and courage. But her no-nonsense, bold, and bossy attitude that we all feared and respected had faded.

She was weakening more each time we saw her. And then, one day, she turned her back on her beloved bowl of treats and walked away without a glance.

That day, we knew it would be the last meal we would ever prepare for her…

Her story, both wild and wondrous, is shared in my second book, *The Elephants of Thula Thula*. Frankie wasn't just any elephant. She was born to lead, and her loss didn't just break our hearts – it sent the entire herd into confusion.

When a pillar like Frankie falls, everything collapses.

For me, it has never been the same without you, Frankie.

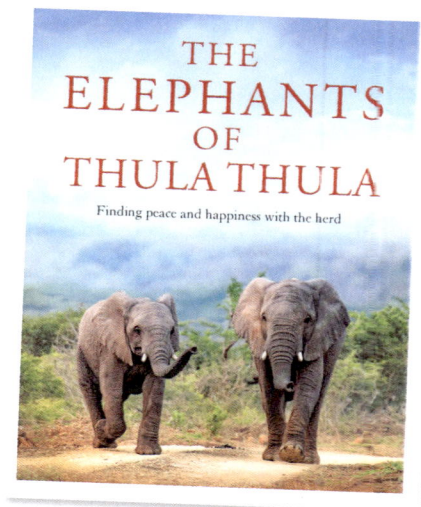

Numzane's story

After the grand garden visit from Nana and the original gang of seven, Numzane decided he preferred a more exclusive audience.

So, naturally, he showed up at the house... alone.

Numzane came with baggage (and not the kind you pack). His mother was the original matriarch, before the legendary Nana took over. A brilliant escape artist, she made it her mission to turn game reserve gates into revolving doors. Unfortunately, her frequent jailbreaks led to annoyed farmers and, in a tragic twist, she and her baby were shot just before the herd was relocated to Thula Thula.

And so, Numzane arrived orphaned. A bit of a misfit. An outsider with attitude. Naturally, he turned into something of a rebel and troublemaker.

One sunny afternoon, while sipping tea on the veranda with a visiting local Chief and Lawrence, we noticed Numzane wandering about near the Chief's open bakkie, which was parked just on the other side of the fence. It was end-of-the-month Friday (shopping day) and the Chief had clearly gone big – bags of oranges, sacks of sugar, huge bags of maize meal, trays of eggs. Basically, the elephant equivalent of a five-star buffet.

Numzane's eyes lit up. You could practically hear his internal monologue: "Well, well, well ... What do we have here?". Before anyone could say, "Stop, thief!", Numzane had his trunk in the loot. Oranges went rolling down the parking area like runaway bowling balls. He smashed the bags of sugar with his foot and even made a huge omelette with all the broken eggs. He made himself very comfortable with the feast and then, as casually as he'd arrived, waddled off happily with a full stomach and maize meal all over him – leaving behind an impressive mess and no regrets.

We just sat there, speechless, teacups frozen mid-air.

To this day, I often wonder how the Chief explained to his wife that the grocery run was hijacked by an elephant.

"Darling, you'll never believe what happened... "

And then came the cheetah

Just when I thought I'd seen it all – elephants in my kitchen, elephants in my garden, elephants on the grocery run – along came Ayana.

There I was, chatting to my office staff by the pool, enjoying a peaceful afternoon, when I spotted her. Ayana, our newly-arrived wild cheetah, was gliding towards my house like she owned the place. Total confidence. Zero hesitation. The same attitude Frankie the Matriarch had when she gate-crashed my garden five years prior. Déjà vu, just smaller with more spots and fewer wrinkles.

After 27 years of living side by side with wild animals, you'd think I'd be unshakable. But I've learnt one thing – none of them know their actual size. My doggies – bless them – have the bravery of lions and the wisdom of slices of toast. They'd have gone after Ayana like she was a trespassing pigeon, entirely unaware they were challenging the fastest land mammal on Earth to a duel.

Cheetahs do not eat dogs, I was told. Well, OK, that's a relief. By the way, they do not eat humans either. Good to know.

Now, Ayana came from 20,000 hectares of pure wild land – no people, no fences.

A wild cheetah with no prior human experience. So her bold little strut towards my house felt like watching a National Geographic episode with me in it.

Naturally, I did what any rational human would do. I grabbed my phone. This is going to be great on Instagram, I thought. I was filming her elegant prowl, silently wondering if the 10,000-volt electric wires around the garden would act like a polite 'No Entry' sign.

Well, no, they did not.

She just stepped right over them like it was a yoga mat. That's when panic set in.

"No, Ayana! Stop now!" I shouted.

She stopped, looked at me like, as in "Who are you?", then turned around and trotted off.

Naturally, I took full credit for this retreat and immediately dubbed myself 'The Cheetah Whisperer'. Though in reality, I think I just startled her with my sudden human squawking.

But hey, a win is a win.

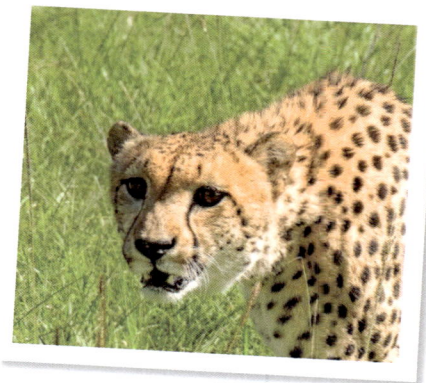

Welcome to the Elephant Safari Lodge, where the wild really means wild!

At the Elephant Safari Lodge, every arrival is a grand entrance, and not just for our human guests. On this particular day, Mabona, our ever-gracious safari lodge manageress, was preparing a warm welcome for a group of American travellers. With the finesse of a seasoned host, she lined up twelve stunning champagne glasses on the bar, each one filled with a vibrant and colourful cocktail – an exotic blend of fruit juice and granadilla syrup. It was a rainbow in a glass.

But while Mabona and the hostesses made their way to the lodge entrance to greet the incoming guests, a few uninvited VIPs had other plans. Enter: the monkey mafia.

Just minutes later, as the guests stepped into the bar area, they were greeted not with clinking glasses, but the crash of shattered crystal and the sight of a cheeky troop of monkeys making a swift getaway – tails in the air and juice on their whiskers. The bar looked like the aftermath of a very wild cocktail party… with no humans in sight.

It was, undoubtedly, an unforgettable first wildlife encounter.

And little did our guests know that this was just the welcome drink. The real adventure had barely begun.

Monkey breakfast

This is the favourite moment for those clever little primates. Guests returned from the morning safari around 08h30 in summer and 09h00 in winter.

Tables with white cloths are beautifully set up and a buffet with croissants, banana bread, and fruit salad is on display for our guests. But up in the trees, a different kind of guest is watching. And they're not here for the view.

This is when the game starts at the safari lodge or at the tented camp.

One staff member, spray bottle in hand, stands guard at the buffet table – a lone so dier fending off a battalion of banana bandits. But let's face it, we humans like to think we're the smarter species.

That illusion usually lasts right up until a monkey swoops down like a ninja and vanishes with a croissant before anyone can say "bon appétit".

The monkeys have already spotted the distracted guest talking to his friends at the breakfast table, and in a quarter of a second, coming from nowhere, the croissant or banana bread has vanished from the guest's plate.

Always fun to watch us running towards the culprit, who is perched on a tree branch above us by then, devouring his croissant and observing us, the clever humans, with amusement as we scramble below.

One particularly sophisticated monkey once snatched a chocolate croissant with a napkin. Yes, really. Having clearly picked up a thing or two about etiquette, he devoured the pastry – chocolate smears and all – and daintily tossed the napkin back to the ground when he was done.

How thoughtful.

Lesson of the day? Never underestimate a monkey with a taste for *pâtisserie*. And maybe, just maybe, we humans still have a thing or two to learn.

Gourmet elephants

One late afternoon, our herd decided to visit us at the safari lodge, as they often used to when their roaming land was smaller. We were only 1,000 hectares at that time, so we used to 'bump' into them often between the lodge and the house, with them creating interesting 'roadblocks', and always a good excuse to be late for work.

Now, Thula Thula has grown to 5,000 hectares and our 28-elephant herd has so much more land to explore. But we miss their regular visits to the lodge or the tented camp.

It's always an immense pleasure for our guests to observe them from the veranda, especially now that we've fenced off the lodge area to keep them from wandering in as they once did. Then again, with this special herd, nothing is ever certain. If you know their history here at Thula Thula – arriving in 1999 and quickly playing escape artists – you'd also know that if they really want to come in… well, let's just say no fence is ever entirely elephant-proof.

So that day, I was in shock when I saw a guest walking down from the Suite Royale with two mangoes in his hands, approaching the elephants. Of course, they LOVE mangoes, our babas.

They looked at our guest and his fruits with a strong interest as he came closer to them. The shouting from the veranda of the lodge and two rangers running towards our guest startled him, but also stopped him from a probable (fatal) trampling.

Thinking that wild animals are pets, particularly when they weigh between two and five tonnes, is not a good idea. Those were wild elephants and are not supposed to be approached too closely, or touched or kissed. A cat or a dog, yes. Not a wild elephant.

So, the next time you're tempted to offer your lunch to an elephant, remember: admire from a distance. Or you might end up the one being served.

Numzane, our charismatic and camera-loving bull, was more than just one of Thula Thula's biggest boys – he was a full-blown celebrity. He was posing like a top model or pretending to climb up a tree to reach the last leaf at its top. Guests would approach him on foot, close to the fence, to photograph our big star. Numzane worked the crowd. Until the guests had taken enough photos and walked back up to the lodge.

Observing Numzane's reaction, looking so confused, watching the guests walking away from him, was hilarious, as if he was saying "Hey, I'm still here, look at me!"

But that was after we had fenced off the lodge area to stop the bold visits of the herd. So, at least he could not run after them to the lodge.

Before then, we had a few adventures that could have ended up problematic. It convinced us to take that decision to protect staff and guests. And trees. Because once upon a time, before the fence, Numzane took 'room service' a little too literally.

One late afternoon, just before dinner, we saw Numzane approaching the entrance of our executive suite, the Suite Royale. There was a marula tree there, too. It was a great spot to settle down for dinner, eating the favourite fruits of the elephants, picking them one by one with their trunks. Numzane was going to be there for a while. Our honeymooners staying in that suite were unaware of the situation, and we called them via the intercom to inform them NOT to open their front door, as there was an elephant standing there.

We heard a giggle, and then the door opened, followed by a shout in whatever language it was, and the door banging. And silence. Numzane carried on as if nothing happened. It was dinner time and our guests were stuck. We had to send a game ranger to evacuate them from the front veranda door, running towards the dining area, about 20 metres away.

A honeymoon to remember...

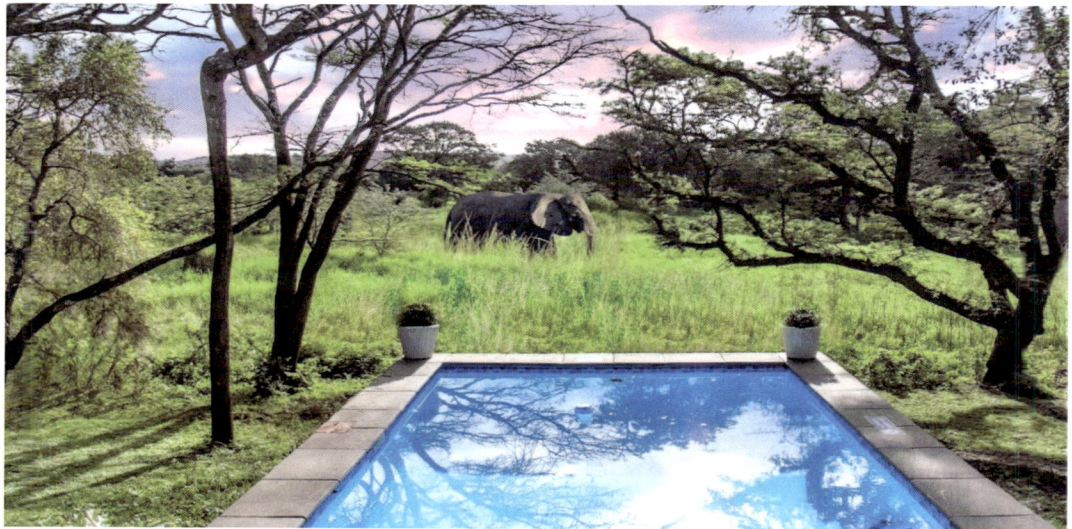

Cheetah panic

Our first female cheetah, Savannah, freshly released from the boma, the enclosure where she had spent several weeks adjusting to her new environment, went straight to the safari lodge, where she caused total panic among the once-peaceful wildlife grazing on the lodge grounds and the humans, whom I had totally forgotten to warn of her release. Oops…

Realising my mistake, I rushed to the lodge and saw the gardener hiding behind a tree, and all my hospitality staff hiding behind the bar or locked up in the kitchen, in panic.

I reassured them as cheetahs do not attack humans; she was just looking for food. Savannah had far better options than them with the large number of antelopes we have at Thula Thula. She was just exploring and simply checking out the antelope buffet, free-range style, from the entrance of our Suite Royale.

Now, our new cheetah girl, Ayana, which means 'wild flower' in Swahili, has also decided to use the safari lodge as her new hunting ground.

Everyone has to eat, we understand that, but she has more than 5,000 hectares of land available to her to find her perfect lunch. Well, seems like she is fond of our safari lodge area, where many impalas, nyalas, and other species enjoy the peaceful atmosphere of this protected space.

Our guests in Suite Royale saw her from their veranda, comfortably stretching in front of them, not bothered by all the cameras and eyes on her. Then, they watched her chasing a young antelope who had, quite unfortunately, wandered into the wrong corner of the garden at the wrong time.

Slightly traumatic for the guests. Wildly educational. 100% nature.

While our rhinos and elephants may be vegetarian, predators like cheetahs play a vital role in balancing the ecosystem. And with only around 1,300 cheetahs left in South Africa (and a mere 6,500 in the world), these elegant hunters are a precious, vanishing thread in the rich tapestry of the wild.

We protect them fiercely. Even if it means the occasional breakfast panic or spontaneous wildlife encounter at the Suite Royale.

At Thula Thula, even the predators check in with style.

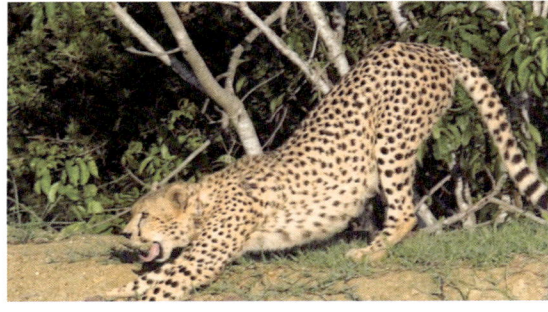

Chef's school at Lenôtre in Paris

I was never a chef. I knew how to cook a meal like everyone else but cooking for a restaurant was another game.

We all must learn the basics in whatever we wish to excel, so I took some classes with the greatest chefs at the renowned French cooking school Lenôtre in Paris. I quickly realised I had a lot to learn if I wanted to teach my kitchen staff how to cook. And learning to adapt French cuisine to a sub-tropical climate with local supplies was going to be an interesting exercise.

Learning the basics was fundamental and required lots of practice, many trials and mistakes, and starting again. Hard work and perseverance, this is how it works, in whatever you want to achieve in life.

A powerful reminder that mastery begins with humility and persistence. I had to learn to be able to teach. And so I did.

> " The greatest lesson I have learnt in life is that I still have a lot to learn. "

Breakfast

Croissant with scrambled eggs and smoked trout

Scrambled eggs and biltong on potato rosti

Egg nest with spinach and parmesan

Soufflé omelette

Eggs en cocotte with mushrooms and white truffle oil

Croque Madame

Pumpkin rusks

Malva pudding rusks

Croissant with Scrambled Eggs and Smoked Trout

serves 1

Ingredients

1 croissant

2 eggs

1 tbsp butter

Pinch of salt and pepper

30g smoked trout

Chives or parsley to garnish

Instructions

1. Prepare the scrambled eggs, cooking them slowly in a non-stick pan. Melt butter over medium-high heat until foamy. Add the eggs and cook, stirring and scrambling gently with a spatula, until fluffy curds form and eggs are fully cooked through. About 3 minutes.

2. Add pepper and a very small pinch of salt, as the smoked trout is usually quite salty.

3. Cut the croissant in half, fill it with the scrambled eggs, and add the smoked trout.

4. Sprinkle with chives or parsley before serving.

Et voilà! A very easy dish to impress your gourmet friends.

Scrambled Eggs and Biltong on Potato Rosti

serves 4

Ingredients

2 medium potatoes

4 eggs

2 tsp olive oil

1 tbsp butter

30g of chopped biltong

Salt and pepper, to taste

Instructions

1. Peel and grate the potatoes. Add salt and pepper.

2. Shape the potato rosti into 8 circles, each about 7cm in diameter and 1cm thick.

3. Place the rosti in a pan and fry in olive oil until crispy and golden on both sides. Remove from the pan and let it cool. If they are too fatty for your taste, use a paper towel to sponge the fat off.

4. Prepare the scrambled eggs, cooking them slowly in a non-stick pan. Melt butter over medium-high heat until foamy. Add the eggs and cook, stirring and scrambling gently with a spatula, until fluffy curds form and eggs are fully cooked through. About 3 minutes.

5. To serve, take a round mould (6cm high and 6cm diameter). Put the mixture in the mould. Carefully remove the mould.

6. Sprinkle with the chopped biltong.

A very simple preparation with a special effect and originality.

Egg Nest with Spinach and Parmesan

serves 1

Ingredients

1 egg

50g fresh spinach

½ clove of peeled garlic

5g parmesan

5g butter

Finch of salt and pepper

Instructions

1. Preheat the oven to 210°C on a ventilated grill.

2. Remove the spinach stem if necessary. Wash and dry the spinach leaves.

3. Melt the butter in a pan and add the garlic. When foamy, add the spinach. Season with salt and pepper and cook for 2-3 minutes. Place the spinach in a buttered ramekin.

4. Separate the egg whites from the egg yolks. Add a pinch of salt to the egg whites and whisk them into stiff peaks. Fold in the grated parmesan.

5. Drop the mixture into a dome in the ramekins. Make a hole in the middle using an empty eggshell. Put the ramekins in the oven for 4-5 minutes. Take them out of the oven and place the egg yolk in the middle of the white. Return to the oven for 2 minutes and serve hot.

Soufflé Omelette

The soufflé omelette of the Mère Poulard is a legendary speciality that made her restaurant, La Mère Poulard, in Mont Saint-Michel famous. This iconic dish is known for its airy texture and lightness, resulting from cooking to perfection. The original recipe dates from the 19th Century and has been well-guarded and still remains a secret. Discover how we, at the Elephant Safari Lodge, prepare this soufflé omelette, as spectacular as it is delicious!

serves 2-3

Ingredients

6 eggs

50g butter

100g grated cheese (emmental, gruyère, or cheddar)

1 tbsp of milk (20ml)

120ml liquid (or pouring) cream

Pinch of salt and pepper

30g bacon (optional)

1 tbsp of chopped fresh chives

Instructions

1. Separate the egg whites from the egg yolks. Place in two separate bowls.
2. In the bowl containing the yolks, add the milk, grated cheese, salt and pepper. Mix well until you get a homogeneous preparation. Stir in the chives.
3. Beat the egg whites with a pinch of salt until they're firm and form peaks. Be careful not to overbeat them as they can become dry.
4. Whip the liquid cream.
5. With a spatula, gently incorporate the egg whites and the cream into the egg yolk mixture. Use movements from bottom to top to preserve the lightness of the mixture. Mix gently until the dough is homogeneous.
6. Pour the mixture into the buttered pan. Cook for about 5 minutes at a low temperature.
7. Serve the omelette soufflé immediately, folding it onto a plate.

This recipe can also be done in a ramekin as a soufflé, using the oven's turning heat and grill. In the ramekin, pour the mixture, then add the pieces of bacon and the grated cheese. Bake for 5 minutes.

Egg En Cocotte with Mushrooms and White Truffle Oil

serves 1

Ingredients

20g mushrooms

2 eggs

1 teaspoon olive oil

1 teaspoon truffle oil

10g butter

Salt and pepper

Instructions

1. Fry the mushrooms in olive oil.

2. Butter the bottom of the ramekin.

3. Break two whole eggs into the ramekin and add the mushrooms.

4. Add salt and pepper.

5. Cook in a bain-marie (water bath) for about 10 minutes.

6. Before serving, add a spoonful of truffle oil for a sublime flavour.

Croque Madame

serves 1

Ingredients

20g butter
30g flour or 15g Maizena
300ml full-fat or whole milk
A pinch of cayenne pepper
A pinch of nutmeg
½ teaspoon Dijon mustard

2 slices of bread
Salt and pepper
1 egg
30g cheddar cheese (or gruyère, mozzarella, gouda)
30g bacon
Parsley or chives for garnish

Instructions

make the roux

1. Melt the butter in a saucepan set over medium heat. Stir in the flour. Cook for 1-2 minutes until the roux turns a light golden brown.

2. Whisk in the milk, a little at a time, until the sauce is smooth and the milk has been incorporated.

3. Reduce the heat and allow to simmer gently, stirring regularly, until the sauce is smooth and thick.

4. Add the spices, 15g of cheese, and mustard. Whisk and season to taste.

make the sandwich

1. Butter each slice of bread on one side. Put both slices butter-side down in the pan on a medium heat.

2. Add 10g of grated cheese on one slice of bread.

3. Fry the bacon and cut into small pieces.

4. Add the bacon on top of the cheese and place the other slice of bread on top.

5. Remove the sandwich from the pan and place it in an oven dish.

6. Add the béchamel sauce over the sandwich, followed by 5g grated cheese.

7. Put in the oven and grill for 3 minutes.

8. Fry the egg in a pan.

9. Remove the sandwich from the oven and place on a hot plate.

10. Top up with the fried egg and sprinkle with pieces of bacon and some herbs to garnish.

This is a big favourite with our guests. Quite a substantial breakfast and maybe a bit rich, but so delicious that one of our guests from the UK asked for it not only for breakfast, but also for lunch and dinner. Every day. Now, I take that as a compliment!

Pumpkin Rusks

Ingredients

1kg self-raising flour

5g salt

500g butter

400g sugar

250ml buttermilk

250ml pumpkin puree

2 eggs

50g pumpkin seeds

Instructions

1. Heat the oven to 180°C.

2. Butter a large dish (I use a large, flat oven-roasting pan) or 2 bread pans (about 18 x 12cm).

3. In a large bowl, add the flour, salt, and butter (cut up into small pieces). Mix well together until it feels like breadcrumbs.

4. Add the sugar and mix well.

5. In a separate bowl, combine the buttermilk, pumpkin puree, and eggs. Beat well together. Add to dry ingredients. Mix everything together well.

6. Scoop into the pan and spread evenly. Bake for 1 hour.

7. Take the pan from the oven and let it cool down before cutting or breaking up the mixture into rusk sizes.

8. Put the cut rusks into the oven to dry them overnight for about 7-8 hours at 80°C.

Malva Pudding Rusks

serves 15

Ingredients

250ml cake flour

250ml white sugar

250ml full cream milk

2 tbsp apricot jam

2 tbsp butter

1 egg

1 tsp bicarbonate of soda

1 tbsp white vinegar and a pinch of salt

Instructions

1. Heat the oven to 180°C and butter a baking dish (30 x 10cm).

2. Mix the flour, sugar, egg, milk, jam, and bicarb together.

3. Add a pinch of salt.

4. Add 1 tablespoon of white vinegar.

5. Pour the mixture into the buttered baking dish.

6. Bake for 45 minutes at 180°C.

7. Dry out in the oven overnight for about 7-8 hours at 80°C.

Swimming with baboons

I always love to watch as playful young baboons dive into the water, showcasing their agility and joy! A heartwarming display of primal playfulness. But…

Our baboons can be quite invasive when they decide to squat at the swimming pool of our exclusive Suite Imperiale.

One guest told me that as she opened her sliding door in the morning, she saw a baboon sitting comfortably on one of the deckchairs. Her first reaction was to close the door and hide, watching the uninvited visitor from inside the room. And wait until he decides to move on. We are in wildlife territory after all. The baboon could argue that he was there long before us humans decided to invade their land with our buildings. And he would be right.

It is never just one or two, but a whole troop enjoying their water aerobics, jumping in the pool while others decide to eat our decorative plants around the pool.

We always recommend that our guests in the suite close their doors when they leave the room, especially if they have snacks inside. Those naughty darlings would not hesitate to invade the suite. And finding a baboon lying on your bed… Well, no.

One morning, while greeting guests at breakfast, a lady told me that a baboon stole her swimming costume that was drying on one of the loungers. I called the gardener of the lodge and asked him, if he sees a baboon in an orange costume, to please ask him to return it to its owner, showing the guest to a very confused gardener. Needless to say, we never found the culprit or the costume.

Baboons are not dangerous to humans. I have learnt, as they often come into my garden, and as I need to protect my doggies, to scare them off by lifting my arms and shouting at them, making myself bigger than them. And it works! Every time.

Back from safari

Some fun stories and a touch of wild unpredictability that only elephants can deliver!

It is always fun to meet our guests coming back from a game drive and listen to their stories about their 'bush adventures', proudly showing their photos and videos.

More monkey fun

Our guests staying in Suite Royale went on an excursion to Hluhluwe Imfolozi Game Reserve. On their way back, they bought a nice selection of fruit from the roadside stall.

They were warned back at the lodge by Mabona to make sure all their windows and doors were closed while they went on the afternoon game drive.

When our guests returned, they informed Mabona that they would not have dinner that evening, as they just wanted a light dinner with the fruits they bought at the market.

So, they asked for a knife and some plates.

Mabona replied that, unfortunately, they had some visitors. One window was left open, and a big joyous party took place in their suite. Just imagine a whole troop coming in and discovering a superb selection of fruits, just for them! That was a five-star dinner for those little bandits, which they enjoyed thoroughly. They also left a horrendous mess behind, as they usually do.

Despite the chaos, we can't help but love these cheeky little thieves. Living in the bush means sharing space with some very clever (and very opportunistic) neighbours. It's all part of the adventure – and a reminder to keep the temptation behind closed windows.

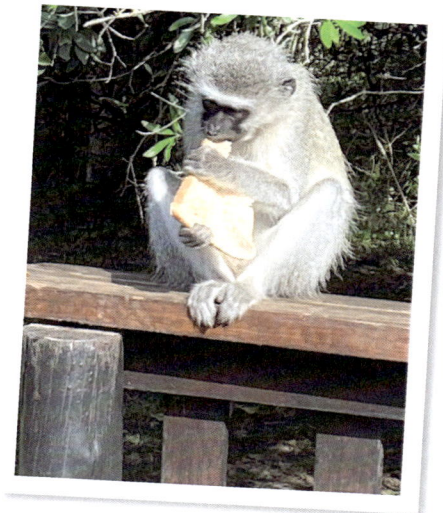

Curious elephant and the cellphone

A guest dropped her cellphone while taking a video of the herd. Bad move. One elephant grabbed it with its trunk and turned it around, trying to figure out what this human's toy was all about. Luckily, it did not ring at that time. He put it to his mouth and decided it was inedible. So, with no use for him, he dropped the cellphone to the ground. The other elephants started playing soccer with it, kicking it to each other. The owner of the cellphone begged the elephants to give it back, but her whispered begging did not work. We never found the cellphone.

Mabona and the blanket heist

One of the funniest stories was when Mabona (not our manageress, but our young female elephant named after her) stole the blanket from one of our guests during the game drive. In winter, it gets chilly on morning or evening game drives, so we provide blankets for our guests. Mabona chose an animal print one and played with it for a while, throwing it in the air and as it landed on her head, repeated her fun game. Meanwhile, our guest was freezing, too shy to ask for his blanket back.

Nana the cooler bandit

Guests were so excited when they witnessed our legendary Nana open the cooler box where drinks and snacks were stored for the sundowner stop during the safari. Everyone was amazed by her incredible ability with her trunk and one tusk to open the cooler box, then forage inside for some tasty bits. This is right beside the stunned game ranger in the driving seat. Everyone watched in total silence.

At least she did not grab the whole box like she did with another game ranger, who had his cooler bag at the back of his vehicle. Nana just took the bag with her trunk and smashed it on the ground, out of frustration, as she could smell something interesting in it, but could not open the zip of the bag.

Another lost cooler box. A brand new one, by the way.

Soups

HOT SOUPS

French onion soup

Curried courgette soup

Vichyssoise with white truffle oil

CHILLED SOUPS

Exotic fruit gazpacho with Amarula

Chilled cucumber soup

Chilled tomato and basil soup with avocado sorbet

BREADS

Grissini with parmesan and olives

Thula Thula secret bread

French Onion Soup

serves 4

Ingredients

4 large onions, thinly sliced
2 tbsp butter
1 tbsp olive oil
2 garlic cloves, minced
1 tsp fresh thyme (or ½ tsp dried thyme)
1 bay leaf
2 cups chicken broth (or vegetable stock)
1 cup dry white wine (optional)
Salt and pepper to taste
8 slices of baguette or French bread, toasted
1½ cups shredded Gruyère

Instructions

1. Melt butter with olive oil in a large pot over a medium heat. Add the sliced onions and cook for 30-40 minutes, stirring occasionally, until they are caramelised and golden brown.

2. Add the minced garlic, thyme, and bay leaf. Cook for another minute.

3. Pour in the chicken broth and white wine (if using). Bring the soup to a boil, then reduce the heat and let it simmer for 15-20 minutes. Season with salt and pepper to taste.

4. Preheat the grill in the oven at 180°C. Ladle the soup into oven-safe bowls. Place a toasted slice of bread on top of each bowl of soup and sprinkle with shredded Gruyère.

5. Place the bowls under the grill for 2-3 minutes until the cheese is melted and bubbly.

6. Carefully remove the bowls from the oven and let them cool slightly before serving.

Curried Courgette Soup

Ingredients

500g courgettes

2 medium-sized potatoes, diced

½ onion

500ml vegetable or chicken stock

60ml liquid cream

1 tbsp cooking oil

1 tbsp curry paste

A pinch of salt and pepper, and a pinch of paprika to garnish

Instructions

1. Fry the onion in cooking oil in a pot at medium heat so the onions do not burn.

2. Add the sliced courgettes and diced potatoes. Cook at a low temperature with the lid on for about 10 minutes, until golden and tender.

3. Add the curry paste, salt and pepper.

4. Add the stock and cook for 45 minutes at a low temperature (do not let it boil).

5. Blend with a food processor until smooth.

6. Pour in the cream.

7. Serve hot with a slice of grilled French bread or a grissini.

Vichyssoise with White Truffle

serves 4

Ingredients

8-10 leeks, chopped

2 large potatoes, chopped

1 onion (or 2 shallots), chopped

20g chives, chopped

1 cup cream (pouring cream)

1 tsp white truffle oil

1 tbsp olive oil with a pinch of paprika

20g butter

Instructions

1. Fry the chopped onions and leeks in butter on a low heat for 10 minutes.

2. Cut the potatoes into cubes and add to the onions and leeks.

3. Continue cooking on a low heat for 40 minutes.

4. Cool down and blend until smooth.

5. Before serving, add the cream and the chopped chives and stir gently.

6. Pour the teaspoon of white truffle oil in the middle of the bowl.

7. Mix olive oil and paprika. Pour it gently on top in a circle for decoration.

8. Serve hot or cold.

Exotic Fruit Gazpacho with Amarula

serves 4

Ingredients

100g of each fruit: pawpaw, pineapple, melon, watermelon, strawberries

8-10 fresh mint leaves

A pinch of cayenne pepper

Cucumber, diced (one big spoon per serving) for garnish

One tot (shot) of Amarula per serving

Instructions

1. Process the fruits and mint in a blender. Leave some fruit aside to cut into small pieces for decoration.

2. Pour into a martini glass.

3. Dice the remaining fruit and use it to decorate the mixture. Pour the Amarula.

4. Serve cold as a starter on a hot summer day.

Chilled Cucumber Soup

serves 4

Ingredients

½ cucumber

1 garlic clove

½ onion

250g plain yoghurt (Greek yoghurt is best)

1 cup of liquid cream

A pinch of paprika and chives for garnish

Salt and pepper

Instructions

1. Cut the cucumber into small pieces.

2. Chop the garlic and onion.

3. Put in the blender and process until smooth.

4. Add the plain yoghurt and the cream. Blend again.

5. Serve in a martini glass and garnish with fresh chives and a pinch of paprika.

Chilled Tomato and Basil Soup with Avocado Sorbet

serves 4

Ingredients

2-3 garlic cloves, crushed

1kg mature rosa tomatoes, chopped

1 avocado

1 tsp fresh lemon juice

15g fresh basil

A pinch of cayenne pepper and salt

1 tbsp olive oil, for frying

Instructions

1. Smash the avocado and add cayenne pepper, salt, and lemon juice. Place in the freezer for 1 hour.

2. Fry the garlic in olive oil for 1 minute. Add the tomatoes and simmer. Cover and cook over a medium to low heat for 45 minutes.

3. Remove from the heat and leave to cool slightly before processing until smooth.

4. Add the basil and pour into a martini glass.

5. Spoon the avocado preparation on top of the soup and garnish with a sprig of basil.

6. Serve with grissini.

The killer tomato soup incident

Our tomato soup has long been a guest favourite. We serve it two ways – steaming hot as a 'cappuccino', with a dollop of whipped cream and a fresh basil leaf, or chilled in a martini glass, topped with a scoop of avocado sorbet. Elegant, simple, and usually a hit.

One evening, I went to greet guests enjoying dinner in the boma. But instead of relaxed, happy faces, I was met with sniffing, coughing, and – alarmingly – teary eyes.

My hostesses were rushing around, handing out tissues. Concerned, I asked what they were eating.

The answer? My beloved tomato and basil soup. What could possibly go wrong with such a classic dish?

I headed straight to the kitchen to investigate and, of course, to taste it myself. One sip later, and I nearly choked. It wasn't soup – it was liquid fire.

A quick check of the ingredients revealed the culprit: habanero. Not a tomato. An ultra-hot chilli pepper. My chef, in an inspired moment of creativity, had decided to spice things up by adding what she thought were peppadews, those sweet, mild, tomato-shaped peppers.

Unfortunately, she'd grabbed a packet of habaneros instead. They do look deceptively similar, but the taste... well, let's just say it's unforgettable.

That night, our tomato soup was a killer – but not in the way I had hoped.

Naturally, I rushed back to the boma with sincere apologies and offered all drinks on the house. Thankfully, our guests took it in good humour (after the burning subsided), and no one pressed charges for attempted murder.

A lesson well learnt: always read the label.

Grissini with Parmesan and Olives

serves 15-20

Ingredients

1 cup of cake flour

1 packet of yeast

1 tbsp of olive oil

½ cup of warm water

½ cup of parmesan

¼ cup of mixed seeds or crushed black olives

Pinch of salt

Instructions

1. Preheat the oven to 180°C.

2. Mix the dry ingredients together.

3. Add the warm water and oil.

4. Mix until the dough is smooth. Add the parmesan and mix well.

5. Add the seeds or the crushed black olives.

6. Set the dough aside for 30 minutes to rise.

7. Roll the dough into small sticks and place them in a tray.

8. Bake in the oven for 20 minutes until it turns golden.

Thula Thula Secret Bread

serves 8

Ingredients

250g cake flour

500g nutty wheat flour

250g bran muffin mix

250g muesli

2 eggs

500g plain yoghurt

1 tbsp of vegetable oil

1 tbsp of baking powder

A pinch of salt

A pinch of cinnamon

Instructions

1. Preheat the oven to 180°C.

2. Mix all the dry ingredients.

3. Add the yoghurt and eggs to the dry ingredients. Mix well.

4. Grease the bread tray (about 25 x 8cm) with vegetable oil.

5. Place in the oven for 45 minutes.

A homemade bread created by my Thula Thula chefs. A true delight.

The healing power of cayenne pepper

When you live in the bush, far from pharmacies and traffic lights, you quickly learn that Mother Nature has her own medicine cabinet – and one of her most fiery little healers is the mighty cayenne pepper.

This tiny red rebel is packed with antioxidants and anti-inflammatory powers that help your body fight off everything from sluggish mornings to aching joints. It gives your heart a boost by improving circulation, wakes up lazy digestion, and – rather miraculously – can even ease pain. (Yes, the same spice that burns your tongue can soothe your muscles. Life's full of surprises.)

And here's the best part – cayenne naturally speeds up your metabolism, which means it helps burn fat. So technically, every time you sip it, you're getting slimmer. I call that guilt-free heat!

Here is my personal detox-and-glow recipe guaranteed to make you feel alive and slightly heroic.

In a large mug, mix:
- ½ teaspoon cayenne pepper
- ½ teaspoon turmeric powder – another golden gem that lowers cholesterol and makes you feel saintly
- A sprinkle of cinnamon – for sweetness, balance, its antioxidant magic and blood-sugar-balancing superpowers
- 1 tablespoon freshly squeezed lemon juice

Fill the mug with boiling water, stir well, and sip slowly (preferably while watching a sunset or an elephant stroll by).

It's bold, it's zesty, and it'll wake up every cell in your body – possibly even the ones that were still asleep from last night's glass of wine.

Cold entrees

NON-VEGETARIAN

Prawn and exotic fruit salad with coconut and chilli sauce

Smoked trout with lemon and chives Chantilly on potato rosti

Couscous and smoked trout salad

Trout and mango tartare

Venison terrine

VEGETARIAN

Tartare of avocado, pawpaw, and pineapple with a honey and balsamic chilli sauce

Tomato and basil tartare on avocado and tapenade toast

Grapefruit, pawpaw, and avocado salad

Prawn and Exotic Fruit Salad
with Coconut and Chilli Sauce

serves 4

Ingredients

for the salad

200g prawns, shelled and deveined (about 50 g per person)
2 kiwis, peeled and sliced
100g strawberries, halved
100g pawpaw or mango (in season), diced
Pineapple, and black and white grapes (quantities as preferred)
1 large avocado, sliced
100g cucumber, diced
A handful of baby rosa tomatoes, halved
Lettuce leaves, for serving

for the sauce

200g prawns, shelled and deveined (about 50g per person)
100ml coconut milk
10g fresh ginger, grated
10g fresh coriander, chopped (plus extra to garnish)
10g fresh chives, chopped
10g fresh chillies, chopped
1 tbsp olive oil
Juice of ½ lemon
Salt and a pinch of cayenne pepper, to taste

Instructions

1. Steam or grill the prawns for 5 minutes, then marinate them with a drizzle of olive oil.
2. Prepare the sauce. In a bowl, mix the coconut milk, ginger, coriander, chives, chillies, lemon juice, olive oil, salt, and cayenne pepper.
3. Arrange the lettuce leaves on plates. Neatly display the prepared fruits, avocado, cucumber, and tomatoes on top.
4. Add the prawns, then spoon over the coconut and chilli sauce.
5. Garnish with extra coriander and seeds of your choice. Serve immediately.

Smoked Trout with Lemon and Chives Chantilly on Potato Rosti

serves 4

Ingredients

120g smoked trout

500ml cream

20g chives, chopped

1 tsp of fresh lemon juice

4 medium potatoes

2 tsp olive oil

Salt and pepper, to taste

Instructions

1. Peel and grate the potatoes. Add salt and pepper.

2. Shape the potato rosti into 8 circles, each about 7cm in diameter and 1cm thick.

3. Place the rosti in a pan and fry in olive oil until crispy and golden on both sides. Remove from the pan and let it cool. If they're too fatty for your taste, use paper towels to sponge the fat off.

4. To make the chives Chantilly, whip the cream until smooth and fluffy. Add lemon juice, chopped chives, salt, and pepper.

5. Marinate the smoked trout with olive oil and pepper.

6. On a plate, place 1 potato rosti, top with the chives Chantilly, then add the smoked trout. Place the second rosti on top as a 'hat'. Garnish with fresh chives.

Couscous and Smoked Trout Salad

serves 4

Ingredients

200g smoked trout

100g couscous

½ yellow pepper, red pepper, and green pepper

½ onion or shallot

1 medium tomato

2 tbsp olive oil

1 tbsp lemon juice

Salt and pepper to taste

Instructions

1. In a large bowl, add 250ml boiling water to the couscous. Cover the bowl with a lid until all the water has been absorbed (usually 15 minutes).

2. Leave the couscous to cool down.

3. Once cooled, dice all the vegetables finely and mix with the couscous.

4. Add salt, pepper, lemon juice, and olive oil to taste.

5. To serve, take a round mould (6cm high and 6cm diameter). Put the mixture in the mould, making it as compact as possible. Carefully remove the mould.

6. Add the smoked trout around the couscous or on top.

7. Serve on lettuce and garnish with parsley or coriander.

Trout and Mango Tartare

serves 2

Ingredients

for the tartare

120g thick piece of trout (not ribbons), lightly smoked

1 small avocado

1 kiwi

4 large strawberries or 8 raspberries

½ mango

for the sauce

10g fresh green chilli, chopped

10g fresh ginger, grated

10g fresh coriander or mint, chopped

4 tbsp olive oil

Juice of ½ lemon

Salt and cayenne pepper, to taste

Instructions

1. Remove the skin from the trout. Cut the fish into small cubes.

2. Cut the avocado, kiwi, mango, and strawberries/raspberries into small cubes.

3. Prepare the sauce by mixing the olive oil, ginger, chilli, lemon juice, coriander or mint, salt, and cayenne pepper.

4. Marinate the trout with the chopped avocado in the sauce.

5. Leave in the fridge for 1 hour, then add half of the chopped fruits.

6. Using a circular mould, shape the mixture and serve on lettuce. Garnish with the remaining fruit and chopped coriander or mint.

Venison Terrine

serves 10

Ingredients

150g bacon

200g pork sausages

400g venison meat, chopped

6 eggs

250ml liquid cream

2 tbsp flour

Whole green peppercorns, to taste

2 garlic cloves, finely chopped

1 onion, chopped

5g thyme

5g chilli

Salt and pepper, to taste

Instructions

1. Lightly fry the bacon, chopped onion, and garlic until slightly golden.

2. Remove the skin from the pork sausages and mash the meat together with the chopped venison in a bowl.

3. Add the eggs and all the spices: green peppercorns, salt, pepper, thyme, and chilli. Mix well.

4. Stir in the cream and mix until fully combined.

5. Transfer the mixture into a terrine dish and let it rest overnight in the fridge.

6. Bake in the oven for 45 minutes.

7. Serve with lettuce, toasted bread, and a fruit kebab to add sweetness and colour.

Risky dinner in the boma - bush magic, mystery, and mischief

Our boma dinners are usually a highlight for our guests – a magical evening under the African skies, lit by flickering candles and accompanied by the gentle sounds of the bush. It's a serene, unforgettable experience.

We've always believed monkeys sleep at night. At least, that's what we were told.

One evening, a lovely guest – a frail, soft-spoken lady in her eighties – was quietly enjoying one of our signature starters, a pawpaw and avocado tartare. Suddenly, out of the dark, a monkey appeared and snatched the tartare right off her plate! It gave her quite the fright – and honestly, it startled all of us. This was completely out of the ordinary. Monkeys are not usually part of the dinner service, especially not at night.

Mabona quickly arranged for a fresh dish to be brought out. Thankfully, the monkey didn't return. Perhaps he was still savouring his stolen starter in a nearby tree…

Next came the main course, seafood kebabs. Now, as far as we know, monkeys aren't particularly fond of fish. But this mysterious little bandit had other ideas. He reappeared, targeting the same guest, and made off with the kebab! Apparently unimpressed with the flavour, he tossed it from a tree moments later. No gratitude, no manners.

What puzzled us most was his choice of victim. Why only this lady? And why was there a monkey active at night at all? The whole thing felt almost… personal. Even more curious is how monkeys behave differently towards men and women. When we, the female staff, try to chase them off, they often hold their ground – staring back boldly, sometimes even confronting us. But the moment a man approaches, they scatter. It's as if they sense who might hesitate, who might be unsure, and they exploit it.

Which leads me to wonder: isn't that a bit like humans, too?

This is what we call at Thula Thula the "bush television"

Tartare of Avocado, Pawpaw, and Pineapple with a Honey and Balsamic Chilli Sauce

serves 6

Ingredients

for the tartare

250g cream cheese (about 1 cup)

1 cup avocado purée

2 fresh avocados, chopped

1 cup pawpaw, cut into cubes

1 cup pineapple, cut into cubes

½ cup cucumber, very finely chopped

10g each of chives, coriander, and parsley, finely chopped

4 tbsp lemon juice

2 tbsp crème fraîche

½ cup sweet chilli sauce

Salt and pepper, to taste

for the honey and balsamic chilli sauce

1½ tsp chopped chilli or chilli flakes

1 tbsp honey

2 tbsp balsamic vinegar

1 tbsp olive oil

Mixed herbs, to taste

Seeds and fresh coriander, to garnish

Instructions

1. In a bowl, mix the cream cheese with half of the chives, coriander, crème fraîche, 1 tablespoon lemon juice, salt, and pepper. Set aside.

2. In a separate bowl, combine the avocado purée with chopped avocado, chopped cucumber, parsley, chilli, and 1 tablespoon lemon juice.

3. Mix the pawpaw and pineapple with the sweet chilli sauce, 2 tablespoons lemon juice, coriander, and olive oil.

4. Using a 7cm high circular mould, layer the tartare: first, the cream cheese mixture at the bottom; then the pawpaw, followed by the pineapple; finally, top with the avocado mixture.

5. Prepare the honey and balsamic chilli sauce by combining honey, balsamic vinegar, olive oil, and mixed herbs.

6. Spoon about 1 teaspoon of the sauce over the tartare and decorate around the plate.

7. Finish by garnishing with seeds and fresh coriander before serving.

Tomato and Basil Tartare on Avocado and Tapenade Toast

serves 8

Ingredients

for the tartare

8 medium ripe, firm tomatoes
2 shallots, finely chopped
10 basil leaves, chopped
4 tbsp olive oil
2 tbsp balsamic vinegar
Salt, pepper, chilli, and nutmeg, to taste

for the avocado

1 large avocado
1 tbsp lemon juice
Salt and pepper, to taste

for the tapenade

10 black olives
1 clove garlic
1 tbsp olive oil

to serve

8 slices Cape-style bread, toasted
Feta cheese, for garnish
Extra basil leaves, for garnish

Instructions

1. Poach the tomatoes in boiling water for a few seconds. Peel, remove the pulp, and cut into small cubes.

2. Mix the tomato cubes with chopped shallots and basil. Add olive oil, balsamic vinegar, salt, pepper, chilli, and nutmeg. Marinate in the fridge for about 1 hour.

3. Mash the avocado with lemon juice, salt, and pepper until smooth.

4. Prepare the tapenade by blending the olives, garlic, and olive oil until smooth

5. Toast the bread slices and spread the tapenade on top.

6. Drain any excess liquid from the marinated tomato mixture.

7. Using an individual round mould, layer the avocado purée first, then the tomato tartare on top.

8. Garnish with basil leaves and sprinkle some feta cheese. Serve immediately.

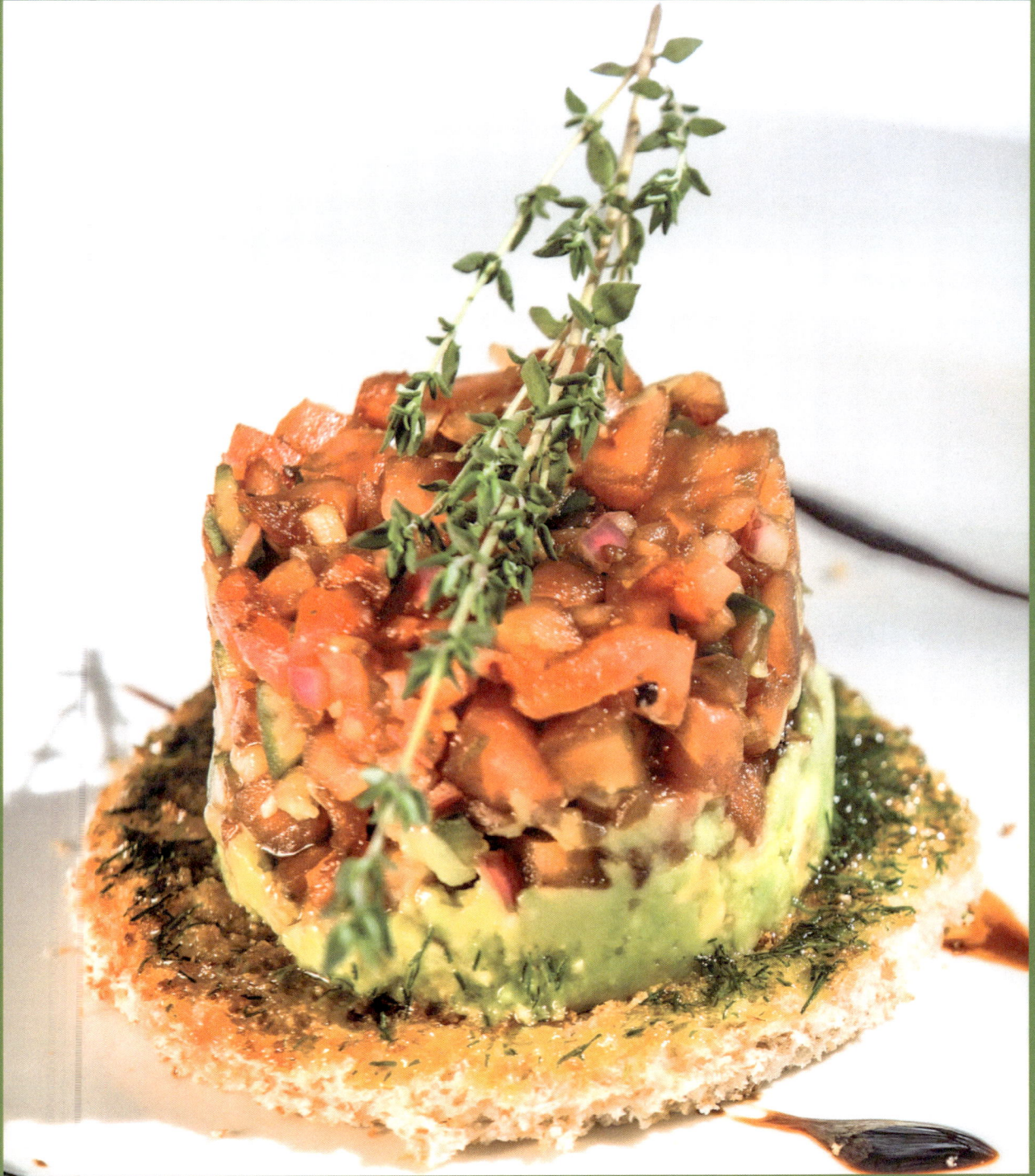

Grapefruit, Pawpaw and Avocado Salad

serves 2

Ingredients

1 avocado
1 grapefruit, peeled and cut into slices
100g pawpaw
50g baby rosa tomatoes, halved
100g cucumber, cut into thin slices
4 olives
30g feta, cut into cubes
4 mint leaves
for the dressing
1 tbsp olive oil
Juice from ½ a lemon
1 tbsp honey
5g fresh chilli

Instructions

1. Cut the pawpaw in half and remove the seeds.

2. Dice the avocado and cut the grapefruit and cucumber into slices.

3. Place the cut fruits in the middle of the halved pawpaw.

4. Add the olives, baby tomatoes, and feta.

5. Prepare the dressing by mixing all the ingredients. Pour over the fruits and vegetables.

6. Garnish with mint leaves.

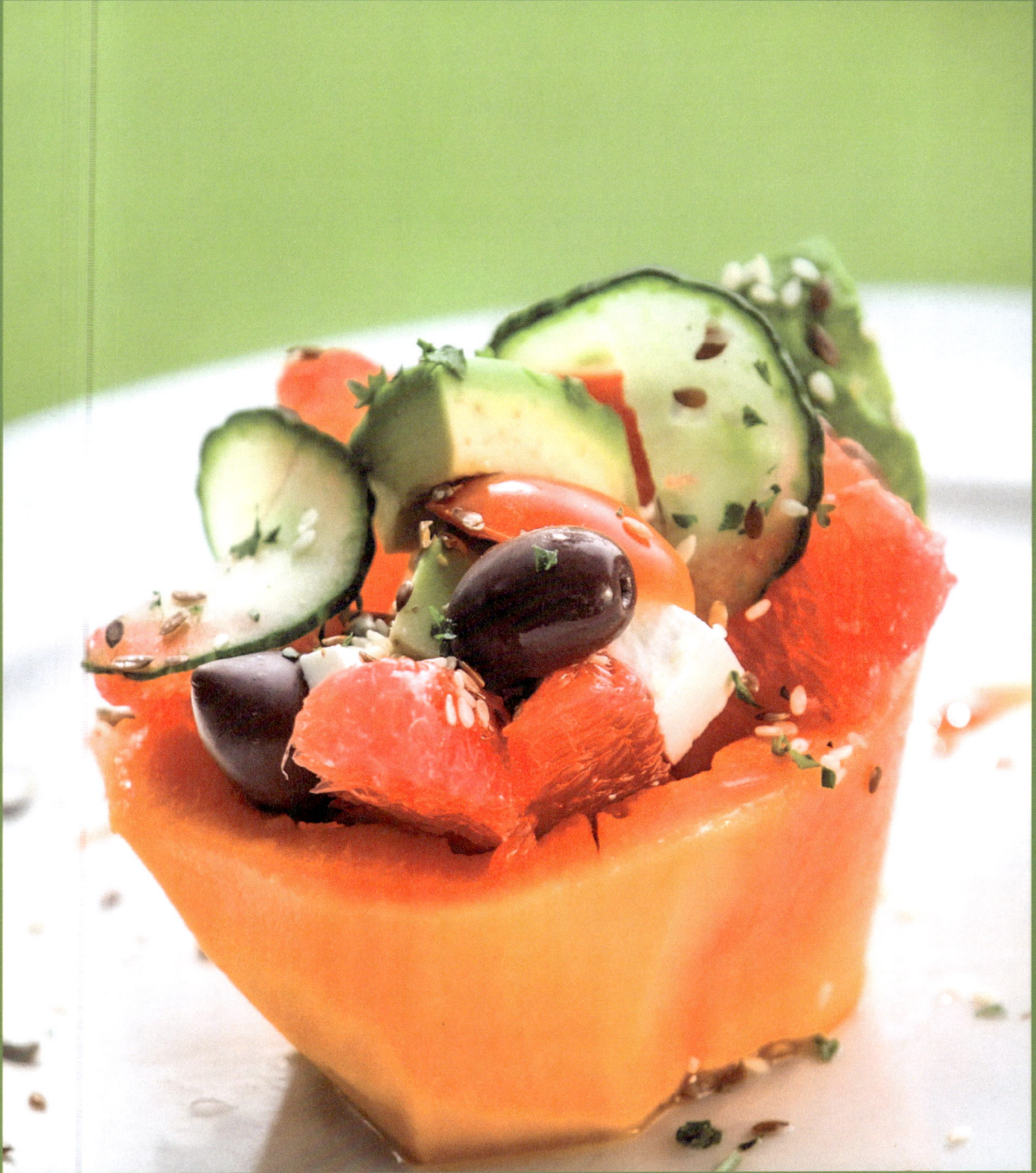

A most refreshing and colourful dish, perfect for Summer.

Dinner with the herd

Dinner at the *Elephant Safari Lodge* was often interrupted when the elephants arrived, much to the surprise of our guests.

In the early days of the lodge, there were no fences stopping our gentle giants from roaming freely within the grounds, leading to a few memorable – and sometimes startling – encounters for staff and visitors.

Elephants love the marula fruit, and we happened to have such a tree just below the veranda of the lodge. One evening during dinner, while guests were happily enjoying their meals under the stars, the elephants decided the marulas weren't enough. Silently, and with great curiosity, they climbed the small incline and stepped right onto the veranda, drawn by the enticing aromas coming from the dinner plates.

A sudden wave of panic swept over us. We quickly ushered guests inside the lodge, where they took cover behind the bar, peeking out at the unexpected dinner crashers. Fortunately, after a few sniffs – perhaps put off by the garlic – they lost interest and ambled away. No damage done, except to our nerves.

That was the moment we realised: as much as we loved the unfiltered wilderness, perhaps it was time to install a fence around the lodge.

Even with the new barrier, the elephants still came to visit, lining up along the fence like curious dinner guests waiting for an invitation. Guests continued to marvel at their presence, now with a safe and respectful distance between them.

One of my favourite memories is of the young elephants, small enough to duck under the wire. Some would attempt to sneak through, only to be gently stopped by their mothers, who would place a trunk across their backs and guide them patiently back to safety. A quiet moment of discipline and love. A dream of all mothers, really.

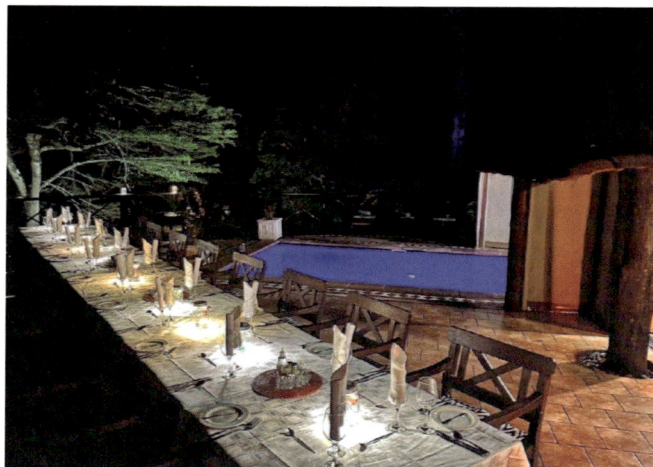

Hot entrees

Mushroom and biltong
vol-au-vents

Three cheese and pesto in
phyllo on tomato compote

Tomato tarte Tatin with pesto
and tapenade

Mushroom and Biltong Vol-Au-Vents

serves 6

Ingredients

for the vol-au-vents

2 rolls ready-made puff pastry
1 large egg yolk, lightly beaten
5ml water (for brushing)

for the béchamel sauce

3 garlic cloves, crushed
30ml butter
30ml cornflour
250ml milk
250ml cream
Salt and freshly ground black pepper, to taste

for the filling

125g brown mushrooms, quartered
125g portobello mushrooms, quartered
50g biltong, finely diced
Olive oil, for frying

Instructions

1. Prepare the vol-au-vents: Cut 18 circles from the puff pastry (about 7cm in diameter). Cut the centres out of 12 discs to form rings, leaving an edge of about 1.5cm. Keep the smaller discs for later.

2. Place the pastry discs on greased baking sheets. Wet the edges with a little water and place a ring neatly onto each disc. Wet the top of each ring slightly and place a second ring on top. Prick the base with a fork and chill for 15 minutes. Chill the smaller discs as well.

3. Mix 5ml water into the egg yolk and brush the mixture onto the pastry. Bake all pastry pieces for 20 minutes, or until golden brown.

4. To make the béchamel sauce: Melt 10ml butter in a pan and fry the garlic for 1 minute. Add the remaining butter. Mix the cornflour into the milk until smooth, then add it to the melted butter. Bring to a boil, stirring constantly to avoid lumps. Lower the heat and cook until thickened. Stir in the cream and season with salt and pepper.

5. Fry the mushrooms in a little olive oil for 3-5 minutes. Add half of the mushrooms and half of the biltong to the sauce.

6. Fill the baked vol-au-vents with the mushroom sauce. Top with the reserved mushrooms, biltong, and a pastry disc. Serve immediately.

Three Cheese and Pesto in Phyllo on Tomato Compote

serves 6

Ingredients

for the phyllo parcels

4 tbsp olive oil

3 garlic cloves, chopped

300g baby rosa tomatoes, halved

60g feta, crumbled

60g mozzarella, diced

60g parmesan, grated

100g basil pesto (basil, pine nuts, garlic, olive oil)

Thyme, salt, pepper, nutmeg,
and a pinch of chopped chilli

Muffin tins, lightly greased with oil

for the tomato compote

4 tomatoes, poached in boiling water
and peeled

2 garlic cloves, chopped

Salt and pepper, to taste

Olive oil, for frying

Instructions

1. Prepare the tomato compote: fry the chopped garlic in a little olive oil, add the peeled tomatoes, season with salt and pepper, and cook over a low heat for 2 hours. Set aside.

2. Preheat the oven. Cut each phyllo sheet into 25cm squares and place each square into a lightly oiled muffin tin.

3. Mix the baby rosa tomatoes, feta, mozzarella, parmesan, pesto, and spices together. Spoon the mixture into each phyllo square.

4. Add a little tomato compote on top of each filling and close the phyllo parcels using kebab sticks.

5. Bake in the oven for 20 minutes, until the phyllo is golden and crisp.

6. To serve, spoon some tomato compote onto the centre of each plate and place a phyllo parcel on top.

7. Sprinkle with extra feta cheese and serve immediately.

Tomato Tarte Tatin with Pesto and Tapenade

serves 6

Ingredients

600g baby rosa tomatoes
100g pesto
100g tapenade
100g feta, crumbled
2 tbsp balsamic vinegar
6 tbsp olive oil
Puff pastry, cut into circles to fit tartlet dishes
6 tartlet dishes
1 egg yolk, lightly beaten (for brushing)
Fresh basil leaves, for garnish

Instructions

1. Preheat the oven to 140°C.

2. In each tartlet dish, mix 1 tablespoon olive oil with a little balsamic vinegar.

3. Arrange the baby rosa tomatoes in the dishes and spread evenly with the tapenade and pesto.

4. Bake in the oven at a low temperature for 30 minutes, until the tomatoes soften.

5. Cut puff pastry into circles to fit the top of each tartlet. Brush the pastry with egg yolk.

6. About 10 minutes before serving, remove the tartlets from the oven and place a puff pastry circle on top of the tomatoes.

7. Increase the oven temperature to 180°C and bake for 10-15 minutes, until the puff pastry is golden and crispy.

8. Carefully invert each tartlet onto a serving plate so the pastry is at the bottom and the tomatoes on top.

9. Serve hot, sprinkled with crumbled feta cheese and garnished with fresh basil leaves.

Seafood in the bush

Although we are situated 45km from the Indian Ocean, in the middle of the wild bush of Zululand, we serve some delicious seafood dishes, all with local fish and crustaceans, prepared with a French touch and local flavours.

One day, a guest gestured to the menu and asked one of my hostesses, "Where is your fish from?" to which she responded without hesitation, "From the sea, ma'am." Well, that made sense indeed.

Prawns are a big favourite with our guests, so, while I was away with my friend, Bella, at my apartment in Durban, we kind of created and experimented with a new recipe – fried coconut prawns. We thought it was such a success that I decided to put it on the menu for Christmas Eve. For Christmas and New Year, we always prepare a five-course feast, and this year, we had a full house. The preparation of the prawns was a bit complicated and it had to be served immediately, hot and crispy. With Bella, we had just done it for the two of us. Now, I had 20 hungry guests waiting for this sublime experiment that I was so proud of.

Cooking 80 prawns at the same time ended up being a bad idea. The smoke coming out of that kitchen! With all of the spices burning our eyes and blinding us with tears (oops, a bit too much chilli), I thought I was setting the kitchen on fire. Mabona and my chefs were in total disarray.

We managed to survive the crisis this disastrous new experiment caused – but that didn't mean I wasn't punished. I was banned from the kitchen for months by Mabona, literally blocking the door of the kitchen each time I was coming up inspired 'with a great creation of a new experiment'.

Very sad that genius can sometimes be misunderstood…

Seafood dishes

Seafood creole in a pancake

Calamari and chorizo in spicy tomato compote

Prawn curry and creamed spinach vol-au-vents

Bouillabaisse creole

Seafood and mushroom gratin

Seafood Creole in a Pancake

serves 6

Ingredients

1kg fresh ripe tomatoes, chopped

200g prawns, peeled and cleaned

100g calamari, cleaned and sliced

1 onion, chopped

1 garlic clove, whole

1 cup coconut milk

20g fresh coriander, chopped

20g fresh ginger, grated

10g fresh chilli, chopped

Fresh thyme, chives and nutmeg, to taste

Salt and pepper, to taste

1 glass white wine (optional)

½ cup lemon juice

Pancakes, to serve (1 per person)

Kebab sticks, for folding pancakes into baskets

Instructions

1. Fry the onion and tomato in a little oil. Add the whole garlic and half of the coriander. Cook for 1 hour.

2. Add the calamari, white wine (if using), lemon juice, more garlic, coriander, chives, and ginger. Cook for 30 minutes.

3. Just before serving, add the coconut milk and cook for 2 minutes.

4. Add the seafood – place the calamari in first, then the prawns. Cook for about 5 minutes, until just done.

5. Serve immediately in pancakes folded into baskets and secured with kebab sticks.

Calamari and Chorizo in Spicy Tomato Compote

serves 4

Ingredients

200g calamari, cleaned and sliced

100g chorizo, sliced

2 tbsp olive oil

15g fresh coriander, chopped

Cayenne pepper, to taste

Salt, to taste

for the tomato compote

4 tomatoes, poached in boiling water and peeled

2 garlic cloves, chopped

Salt and pepper, to taste

Olive oil for frying

Instructions

1. Prepare the tomato compote: Fry the chopped garlic in a little olive oil. Add the peeled tomatoes and season with salt and pepper. Cook over a very low heat for 2 hours. The longer the better (that's the secret for the best tomato compote).

2. Heat the olive oil in a pan. Grill the calamari and chorizo for about 5 minutes.

3. Stir the grilled calamari and chorizo into the prepared tomato compote. Season with cayenne pepper and salt.

4. Garnish with fresh coriander and serve hot with couscous or rice on the side.

Prawn Curry and Creamed Spinach Vol-Au-Vents

serves 6

Ingredients

200g prawns, deveined and shelled
2 rolls puff pastry
2 tbsp curry masala
1 onion, chopped
(plus 1 extra tbsp finely chopped onion for spinach)
4 garlic cloves, chopped
10g fresh ginger, grated
10g fresh coriander, chopped (plus extra for garnish)

6 ripe tomatoes, chopped
300g fresh spinach
3 tbsp olive oil
150ml coconut milk
1 egg yolk (for pastry)
Salt and pepper, to taste

Instructions

for the tomato curry base

1. Heat 2 tablespoons of olive oil in a pan. Fry the tomatoes, onion, garlic, curry masala, ginger, and coriander.
2. Cook gently over very low heat for 2 hours, stirring occasionally.

for the creamed spinach

3. Heat 1 tablespoon of olive oil in another pan. Sauté the extra onion until soft, then add the spinach.
4. Season with salt and pepper and cook until just wilted.

for the puff pastry vol-au-vents

5. Using an oval cutter, cut 6 pastry shapes. Place on a baking tray and refrigerate for 30 minutes.
6. Brush with egg yolk and bake at 180°C for 15 minutes, until puffed and golden.
7. Once baked, carefully cut each vol-au-vent in half to form two layers.

for the final assembly

8. Add the prawns to the tomato curry base and cook for 1 minute.
9. Stir in the coconut milk and cook for 2 more minutes. Adjust seasoning to taste.
10. To assemble: Place a spoonful of creamed spinach in the bottom half of each pastry, top with prawn curry, then cover with the other half of the pastry.
11. Garnish with chopped coriander and serve hot.

George's story

George was a rescued bush baby, only a few weeks old when we got him at Thula Thula from a rehab centre. We had built a little house for him at the entrance of the lodge. George always enjoyed eating his dinner of fruit with honey, prepared with love by our kitchen staff.

But only after he had a drink at the bar with the guests.

Bush babies being nocturnal, George became a great entertainer at our safari lodge every evening, as guests were returning from the afternoon safari. George loved sweet drinks, and had fun knocking down a can of Coke and licking up the spill from the bar counter. Then, he would jump on the table during dinner, although uninvited, going around, looking for some tasty bits.

George loved prawns. He once grabbed one from the plate of a guest who was unwilling to share it and tried to grab it back. George bit his finger and the guest had no choice but to let George have the prawn. I was told the guest was a well-known rugby player in South Africa, who kind of lost his sense of humour that evening and went to bed with a bleeding finger and a bruised ego. George continued coming back every evening, until he met a bush baby girlfriend that we named Fifi. She was tiny, young, and pretty. She was also wild, not a rescue like George, and was not used to humans, so she was a bit shy. We were happy for George and prepared dinner for two at the lodge.

After meeting Fifi, George never came back to the pub. Typical.

They disappeared, happily ever after and maybe had lots of babies. We could hear their loud cries at night, calling their bush baby friends, and we were happy that George had found a way to be wild at last with his own kind, where he belonged.

Gourmet bush babies

So George and Fifi went off happily to fulfil their life in the wilds, but never too far from the safari lodge. They likely shared their special culinary experiences with their children and grandchildren, because lately, we've noticed some very selective foraging in the lodge kitchen. Specifically, in the cooler room.

True gourmet bush babies, they choose only the best – lemon tart, cooked puff pastry from our vol-au-vents, and mozzarella. They also have a taste for pawpaw and avocado, probably preparing their own tartare… a four-course dinner, just like we serve to our guests.

Those clever little creatures have found a gap somewhere in the thatched roof to get in at night, when no one is watching. However, our kitchen surveillance cameras caught the little connoisseurs red-handed – sniffing, nibbling, and selecting only the finest options available.

But now, there is no more gap in the roof. Thanks to the cameras, we were able to close the weak spot.

So, monkeys during the day and bush babies at night. We're actually creating true gourmet species at Thula Thula. Compliments to the chefs!

Bouillabaisse Creole

serves 6

Ingredients

200g calamari
200g soft blue crab
200g shelled prawns
200g crayfish
4 tbsp coconut powder
100ml coconut milk (not cream)
1kg fresh ripe tomatoes
1 onion, chopped
4 cloves garlic, crushed
20g fresh coriander
20g fresh ginger, grated
10g fresh chilli, finely chopped
½ lemon (juice)
A few sprigs fresh thyme and chives
Pinch of nutmeg
Olive oil (for frying)
Salt and pepper, to taste
2-3 cups white wine (optional)

Instructions

1. Prepare the tomato base: Fry the onions and half of the garlic in olive oil until soft. Add the ripe tomatoes and simmer gently. Stir in half the herbs and spices. Cook slowly over a low heat for 2 hours to develop the flavour.

2. Add a few pieces of calamari to enrich the stock, then pour in the white wine (2-3 cups) and lemon juice. Add more garlic, coriander, chives, and ginger. Simmer for 30 minutes.

3. When ready to serve (before putting in the uncooked seafood), add the coconut milk and simmer for 2 minutes.

4. Add the seafood: Start with the calamari (about 5 minutes), then add the crab and prawns (3 minutes). Finally, add the crayfish and cook just until done.

5. Season to taste with salt, pepper, and nutmeg. Serve immediately while hot.

Tip: The sauce can be prepared in advance and put in the freezer.

Seafood and Mushroom Gratin

serves 6

Ingredients

200g calamari
200g prawns, shelled and deveined
200g firm white fish (eg kingklip), cut into large cubes
200g brown or portobello mushrooms, diced
2 tbsp olive oil
4 garlic cloves, chopped
10g fresh chilli, finely chopped
10g fresh chives, chopped
Fresh parsley, chopped (for garnish)
Salt and pepper, to taste

for the béchamel sauce

50g cornflour
500ml milk
50g butter
½ glass dry white wine

Instructions

1. Preheat the oven to 180°C (fan/grill).

2. Make the béchamel sauce: Melt the butter in a pan, stir in the cornflour, and slowly whisk in the milk until smooth. Add the white wine, chives, salt, pepper, and a little chili if desired. Simmer until thickened.

3. Marinate all seafood with olive oil, salt, and pepper.

4. Grill the calamari for 5 minutes, then add the prawns and fry for 2 minutes in olive oil.

5. Cook the fish cubes separately, frying for about 4 minutes until just done.

6. Fry the mushrooms in olive oil with garlic, chilli, salt, and pepper until tender.

7. In a gratin dish, combine the cooked seafood and mushrooms with the béchamel sauce. Mix gently.

8. Bake under the grill for 10 minutes until bubbling and lightly golden.

9. Garnish with chopped parsley and serve hot.

Chicken and sangoma

We have a Zulu village bordering Thula Thula called Buchanana. This local community is where most of our hospitality staff come from.

We organise for our guests to visit this village as an authentic experience of rural Zulu living. Included in the visit to the village, apart from the school, the shops, and the church, is the encounter with the sangomas, highly respected traditional healers and diviners. Male or female, they are chosen – spiritually – and have the sacred ability to heal through rituals, both physical and emotional. They are also seen as prophets, with the power to read the future. I hadn't met this particular sangoma before, but I know each one has a unique way of practicing.

Our group from the US was very excited to meet with the new sangoma. But when they returned from their excursion to the village, they all looked a bit in shock, as if in a trance, as they all sat silently at the dinner table. The atmosphere, usually joyous with the tales of the day, was that of a funeral.

The ranger who accompanied them and served as a translator, as the sangoma rarely speaks English, told me the interesting story of their experience.

I found out that her rituals as a diviner of the future consisted of calling the ancestors while brutally hacking the throat of a live chicken. In front of the guests.

I understood their state of shock better.

But now the funniest part of the story: Guess what was on the menu that evening for dinner? Roast chicken. We had to make changes quickly before they all started packing and running away.

The sangoma, traditional healer and diviner

Meat dishes

Chicken, pineapple, and chocolate chilli sauce

Chicken madras curry

Blanquette de poulet au vin blanc

Duck cassoulet

Lamb and red wine gratin parmentier

Boeuf en croûte

Fillet of impala with red wine and bacon sauce

Venison bourguignon en croustade

Chicken, Pineapple and Chocolate Chilli Sauce

serves 6

Ingredients

6 chicken fillets
1 pineapple, peeled and sliced
1 tbsp olive oil
3 tbsp sweet chilli sauce
Fresh coriander, chopped
Salt and pepper, to taste

for the chilli chocolate sauce

10g fresh chillies or chilli flakes
1 small onion or 2 shallots, finely chopped
100g dark chocolate, melted
10g coriander seeds
½ glass red wine
1 tbsp olive oil

Instructions

1. Slice each chicken fillet into 3 thin pieces. Marinate with sweet chilli sauce, olive oil, salt and pepper.

2. Grill the chicken slices in a hot pan with a little olive oil until cooked through.

3. Grill the pineapple slices in the same way until caramelised.

4. Prepare the chilli chocolate sauce: Fry the onion in olive oil, then add the coriander seed and chilli. Stir in the melted dark chocolate.

5. Add the red wine and cook gently over very low heat for about 10 minutes until smooth and glossy.

6. To assemble: Place a slice of chicken on a plate, top with a slice of pineapple and spoon over the chilli chocolate sauce. Repeat to create 3 layers.

7. Garnish with fresh coriander and serve immediately.

Chicken Madras Curry
(also for Vegetable or Fish)

serves 6

Ingredients

6 large chicken thighs, cut into cubes (or cubed fish/vegetables of choice)
Juice of 2 lemons
Zest of 1 lemon
350ml yoghurt
300ml liquid cream
10g mustard seeds
15g fresh coriander, chopped
1 tbsp curry powder
2 tsp turmeric
2 tsp cornflour (Maizena)
1 tbsp tomato paste
2 onions, chopped
2 garlic cloves, chopped
Olive oil for frying
Optional: desiccated coconut, for garnish

Instructions

1. Toss the cubed chicken (or fish/vegetables) with the lemon juice. Marinate 10 minutes for chicken or fish, 5 minutes for vegetables.

2. Mix curry powder, turmeric, and cornflour. Coat the pieces evenly.

3. In a pan with olive oil, lightly fry the chicken (or fish/vegetables) and set aside. For vegetables, fry briefly; for fish, fry until lightly coloured.

4. In the same pan, sauté onions, garlic, and mustard seeds until fragrant.

5. Combine tomato paste, yoghurt, cream, and lemon zest in a bowl.

6. Return the chicken (or fish/vegetables) to the pan and gently stir in the tomato-yoghurt mixture.

7. Add fresh coriander and, if desired, a pinch of desiccated coconut.

8. Cooking times: Chicken, simmer for 30 minutes; Fish, simmer for 20 minutes; Vegetables, cook for 5 minutes.

Blanquette De Poulet Au Vin Blanc

serves 4

Ingredients

4 chicken drumsticks
4 chicken thighs
50g celery, diced
100g leeks, sliced
100g onion, diced
100g carrots, diced
100g mushrooms, sliced
4 baby onions, whole
2 garlic cloves, chopped
1 tbsp butter
2 tbsp crème fraîche
2 egg yolks
2 tbsp cornflour (Maizena)
10g fresh coriander, chopped
2 glasses white wine
3 green olives per person
Salt and pepper, to taste

Instructions

1. In a large pan, melt butter and sauté onions, garlic, leeks, mushrooms, celery and carrots for 5-10 minutes. Add the baby onions whole.
2. Add the chicken drumsticks and thighs and cook until golden on all sides.
3. Pour in white wine and add green olives. Season with salt and pepper; simmer for 10 mins.

Prepare the sauce at the last minute

4. In a separate pan, melt a little butter and mix in cornflour, stirring over low heat. Gradually add a small glass of the chicken cooking liquid, then stir in crème fraîche and egg yolks. Cook gently until smooth and slightly thickened.
5. Add the sauce to the chicken and vegetables. Cook for a further 5 minutes on very low heat. Stir gently.
6. Plate with pumpkin and potato purée and sprinkle with fresh coriander.

Duck Cassoulet

serves 6

Ingredients

300g broad dry white beans
6 duck legs and thighs
200g pork rashers, cut into cubes
1 large onion, chopped
4 garlic cloves, chopped
4 tbsp olive oil
2 ripe tomatoes, chopped
2 glasses white wine
Thyme, cayenne pepper, salt and black pepper, to taste
Water as needed

Instructions

1. Soak the beans overnight. Then, precook in water for 2 hours until tender.

2. In a pan, heat 2 tablespoons of olive oil and sauté 2 garlic cloves. Add the chopped tomato and cook over low heat for 2 hours.

3. In a large lidded pot, heat olive oil and fry the chopped onion, remaining garlic, and pork rashers until lightly browned.

4. Add the tomato sauce to the pot and stir well. Add the pre-cooked beans, just covering them with 250ml of water. Cook over a low heat for 30 minutes.

5. In a separate pan, brown the duck legs skin-side down to render fat and achieve a golden colour. Season with salt and pepper.

6. In an ovenproof pot, pour some duck fat at the bottom. Add a layer of beans, then some duck legs, followed by another layer of beans and more duck legs. Cover with the remaining beans.

7. Pour 250ml of water and 2 glasses of white wine over the preparation so the ingredients are just covered.

8. Cook uncovered in the oven at 165°C for about 4 hours.

9. Every 30 minutes, break the crust and baste with the cooking juices. If the dish dries out, add only water as needed.

Lamb and Red Wine Gratin Parmentier

serves 6

Ingredients

500g lamb knuckles

Pink salt and cayenne pepper, to taste

2 glasses (good) red wine

4 tbsp olive oil

6 garlic cloves, chopped

20g fresh thyme

Mashed potatoes (boiled and mashed with butter and seasoning)

To serve: Tomates provençales (see Vegetable section)

Instructions

1. Combine the lamb, red wine, olive oil, garlic, thyme, and pink salt in a covered dish. Marinate for a couple of hours.

2. Preheat the oven to 180°C.

3. Place the marinated lamb in the oven. Reduce the heat to 140°C and cook slowly for about 2 hours.

4. Boil and mash potatoes, then mix in butter and seasonings.

5. Shred the cooked lamb and mix with the red wine sauce to absorb the flavours.

6. In 6 x 6cm rings, layer a spoon of mash at the bottom, then lamb, then cover with more mash.

7. Place under the grill until the top is lightly golden.

8. Plate with tomates provençales on the side.

Boeuf En Croûte

serves 6

Ingredients

800g fillet of beef, cut into 6 slices (2cm thick)
2 rolls puff pastry
300g mushrooms, chopped
2 tbsp Dijon mustard
2 tbsp crème fraîche
100g bacon, chopped
30g butter
4 tbsp olive oil
2 egg yolks (for brushing)
Salt, pepper, and cayenne pepper (optional)
*To serve: Sautéed wild mushrooms and Duchess potatoes, or fried courgette chips
(see Vegetable section)*

Instructions

1. Clean, rinse, and chop mushrooms. Sauté in butter with salt and pepper over high heat until all liquid has evaporated.
2. Fry chopped bacon in a pan until crisp.
3. Preheat oven to 240°C.
4. Unroll the puff pastry and cut into six 15cm squares.
5. In a bowl, combine the fried bacon, mushrooms, Dijon mustard, and crème fraîche.
6. Spread half of the mixture in the centre of each pastry square.
7. Quickly sear the beef slices in hot olive oil for 1 minute on all sides. Season with salt and pepper. The beef should remain very rare.
8. Place the beef on top of the filling. Cover with the remaining mushroom-bacon mixture, spreading evenly around the meat.
9. Brush the puff pastry's edges with egg yolk, fold the pastry over to completely encase the beef, and press the edges to seal.
10. Cut extra pastry pieces and place them on top for decoration. Brush with egg yolk.
11. Bake at a very high temperature for 10 minutes.
12. Reduce the temperature to 190°C. Bake for another 5 minutes until golden brown.
13. Serve hot with sautéed wild mushrooms and Duchess potatoes, or fried courgette chips.

The Thula Thula way!

Fillet of Impala
with Red Wine and Bacon Sauce

serves 4

Ingredients

600g venison fillet (about 150g per person)

2 glasses (good) red wine

1 onion or 2 shallots, chopped

50g bacon, chopped

2 tbsp olive oil

Salt and pepper, to taste

To serve: Sweet potato gratin or Duchess potatoes (see Vegetable section)

Instructions

1. Place the venison fillet in a dish with the red wine, olive oil, salt, and pepper. Marinate for 2 hours.

2. Cut the fillet into 3cm thick pieces.

3. Prepare the sauce: Fry the onion and bacon together until golden. Add red wine and reduce on a low heat for 5 minutes.

4. Grill the fillet pieces in a separate pan over a high heat for 2 minutes on each side. The venison should remain rare.

5. Pour the reduced sauce onto the plate and place the venison fillet on top.

6. Serve with sweet potato gratin or Duchess potatoes.

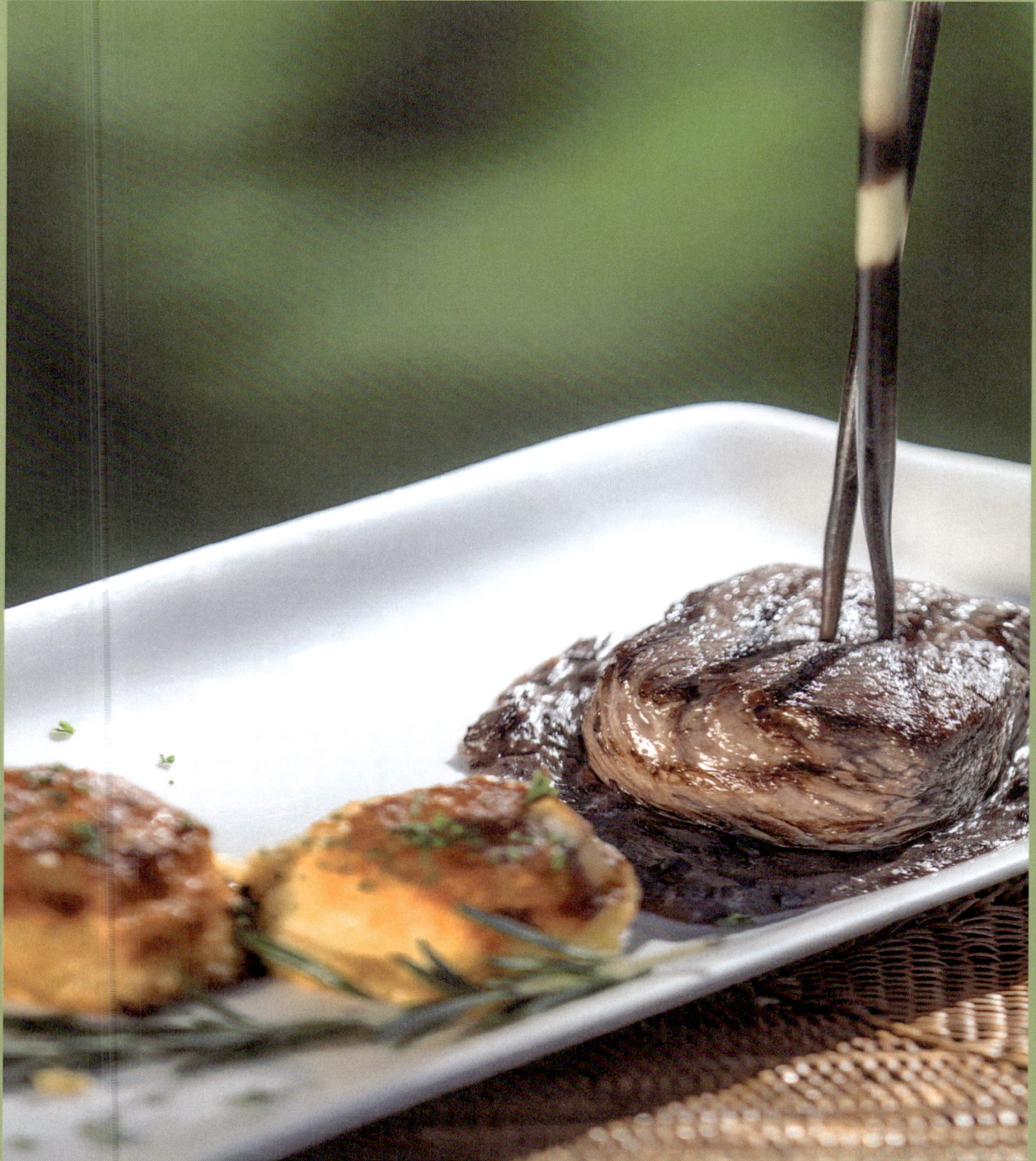

The laws of the wild

To celebrate the expansion of our land to 5,000 hectares in May 2024, we decided to acquire additional species. We had the space, the food, the water. That is, in a nutshell, what animals need.

In October 2024, we welcomed 12 ostriches, and in January 2025, we released our three cheetahs into the game reserve – two males, Amani and Asante, and one female, Ayana. Giving names to our animals gives them a sense of identity. Not just an elephant, a rhino, or a cheetah. It makes them part of the Thula Thula family.

We also received four new hippos to join Romeo and Juliet's big family – Coco, Chanel, Charlotte, and Valentine. Two adult females and two baby girls to balance out the large number of male hippos.

Hippos are no problem as they are vegetarian. Eating grass and plants, just like our elephants and rhinos. Ostriches eat plant-based food, too, and occasionally insects.

But not our cheetahs. They were the first real predators Thula Thula ever had. I mean visible ones, that is, those we actually witness hunting and eating other animals during the day, unlike our hyenas, which hunt at night. The cheetahs catch our small game, such as young nyalas and impalas, which helps to regulate our large number of antelopes, since we do not do any hunting at Thula Thula.

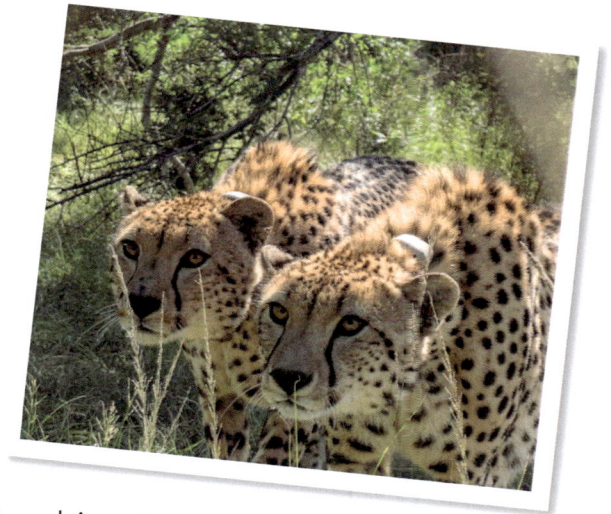

Jerry, Amani and Asante

One ostrich, Jerry, used to come to the house and liked the company of humans. Jerry was friendly and playful, running after our office staff in the garden, trying to get inside the house, driving my dogs mad. The usual fun day in the wilds of Thula Thula.

Jerry also liked to keep our security guard at the main entrance gate company. We liked Jerry.

Until Amani and Asante met Jerry...

The ostrich is the fastest bird and the fastest two-legged animal on land. Their speed can reach up to 70 km/h. But cheetahs are the fastest running animals on earth. Their maximum speed is measured at 115 km/h. Our friendly Jerry did not stand a chance against the two brothers.

Their running competition ended up being probably the most expensive lunch at USD600 an ostrich. Needless to say, we were quite upset with these greedy brothers. We now hope that the remaining 11 ostriches keep their distance from the cheetahs and stick to the safer side of the reserve.

But this is the wild. We don't interfere. We don't control what nature decides. At Thula Thula, we protect, we observe, and we learn. And sometimes, we mourn the quirky characters like Jerry, taken too soon by the laws of the savannah.

Because here, as everywhere in the wild, it's still true: Only the strongest survives.

Venison Bourguignon En Croustade

serves 8

Ingredients

1 leg of venison (eg impala), about 2.5 kg, cut into 2cm cubes
200g pork rashers, diced
2 large onions, chopped
8 baby onions
1 bottle (good) red wine
6 garlic cloves, chopped
300g carrots, sliced
8 baby potatoes
1 tbsp tomato paste
2 tsp flour
2 rolls puff pastry, cut into 20cm rounds
1 tsp nutmeg
Thyme and bay leaves
Olive oil, salt and pepper

Instructions

1. Place the venison cubes in a dish with the red wine, 1 chopped onion, garlic, salt and pepper. Marinate for 6 hours. Reserve the wine marinade.

2. Fry the second onion in olive oil. Add the carrots, baby onions, and other vegetables from the marinade. Cook for 5 minutes.

3. Increase the heat to high and add the venison cubes. Brown for 3 minutes.

4. Sprinkle the flour over the venison and stir constantly.

5. Reduce the heat to low, cover, and cook gently for 20 minutes.

6. Pour in the reserved red wine marinade, stir well, and cook for 2 hours.

7. Once the venison is tender, add baby potatoes and cook for an additional 30 minutes.

8. Cut puff pastry into 20 cm rounds and chill in the fridge.

9. Just before serving, spoon the venison and vegetables into round, ovenproof dishes. Place the puff pastry round over each dish, folding the edges down around the sides. Brush with olive oil. Bake in the oven at 180°C for 15 minutes. Serve immediately.

A rhino love story

When Thabo was just six months old, he strolled confidently around the safari lodge as if it were his forever home. And in a way, it was – at least in his heart.

We always wondered if Thabo, who was only one day old when he was rescued by humans, and who had never seen a rhino before he came to Thula Thula at four months old, thought he was a human or that we were all rhinos.

He was fed at the lodge by our carers, a special milk preparation that he gobbled up with greed, crying to get more. Just like a puppy. Humans rescued him, fed him, and took care of him. Carers were his substitute mother, so the bond was created with humans.

But a wild animal must be reintroduced into the wild to roam freely. That is the principle and the rule for rehabilitating orphans once they are ready for release into the wild. You cannot keep a wild animal as a pet or in captivity, unless it has a health issue.

For many years, Thabo still looked for the company of humans, waiting for a cuddle or just some attention from us, which has made him a big favourite of our guests. Or just standing at the entrance of the safari lodge, wondering why there was now that fence stopping him from coming 'home'.

Now, Thabo is 16 years old and has become rewilded and acts like a 'normal rhino', roaming the vast reserve. Wild animals belong to the wild, with no human interaction apart from observation in their natural surroundings.

Two months after the arrival of Thabo in 2009, a new orphan rescue, a female called Ntombi, became our second rhino to care for at the safari lodge. Ntombi was also the first rhino that Thabo ever met.

Being brought up at the safari lodge always created attraction for our guests. Thabo and Ntombi loved the company of humans. When they were still babies, it was OK. But having a two-tonne rhino on your driveway, stopping you from leaving home, or standing at the front door of a chalet where guests get blocked until our darlings decide to leave, can be a bit of a problem.

We had to 'evacuate' our guests staying in one of the safari chalets through the back window.

Such is life in the bush. Nature always has the last word.

Thabo and Ntombi now live as wild rhinos should – respected, admired from a distance, and most importantly, free.

But every time we see them together, we remember those early days. The babies who once followed us like dogs, who loved back scratches and attention, and who slowly, gracefully, became wild again.

Because love for wildlife means knowing when to let go.

Thabo and Ntombi

Obstacles don't block the path. They are the path.

Vegetable dishes

Tomates provençales

Baked courgette chips with parmesan

Garlic and herb Duchess potatoes

Roasted butternut in phyllo tartlet

Sweet potato gratin Dauphinois

Tomates Provençales

Ingredients

4 tomatoes

2 garlic cloves, finely chopped

50g breadcrumbs

3 tbsp parsley, chopped

3 tbsp basil, chopped

4 tbsp olive oil

Salt and pepper, to taste

Instructions

1. Preheat the oven to 200°C.

2. Cut the tomatoes in half and arrange them cut side up in a baking dish.

3. In a small bowl, mix the garlic, breadcrumbs, parsley, basil, salt, and pepper.

4. Sprinkle the breadcrumb mixture evenly over the tomatoes and drizzle generously with olive oil.

5. Bake for 20-25 minutes in the oven, until the tomatoes are tender and the breadcrumbs are golden.

Baked Courgette Chips
with Parmesan

serves 4

Ingredients

2 courgettes

50g parmesan, grated

50g breadcrumbs

1 egg

Salt and pepper, to taste

Olive oil, for drizzling

Instructions

1. Preheat the oven to 200°C.

2. Wash the courgettes and cut them into sticks to resemble chips.

3. In a bowl, beat the egg with a pinch of salt and pepper.

4. In a separate bowl, mix the breadcrumbs and grated Parmesan.

5. Dip each courgette stick into the beaten egg, then roll in the breadcrumb-Parmesan mixture until evenly coated.

6. Place the coated courgette chips on a baking sheet, drizzle lightly with olive oil, and bake for 20-25 minutes, until golden and crispy.

Garlic and Herb Duchess Potatoes

serves 4

Ingredients

4 medium potatoes, peeled and chopped

2 egg yolks

50g Parmesan, grated

3 tbsp butter

4 garlic cloves, minced

3 tbsp parsley and chives, chopped

A pinch of nutmeg

Instructions

1. Preheat the oven to 140°C.

2. Sauté the garlic in butter for 2 minutes.

3. Boil the peeled and chopped potatoes until tender, then mash them with the butter.

4. Mix the mashed potatoes with egg yolks, parmesan, herbs, sautéed garlic, and nutmeg.

5. Using a piping bag, pipe the potato mixture onto a non-stick baking tray.

6. Bake for 10 minutes. Remove from the oven and brush with melted butter. Return to the oven for another 5 minutes.

7. Garnish with fresh herbs before serving.

Roasted Butternut in Phyllo Tartlet

serves 6

Ingredients

1 butternut squash

A pinch of cinnamon

Salt and pepper, to taste

1 tbsp honey (15ml)

Phyllo pastry, 6 layers

½ cup cream cheese

1 tbsp chives, chopped

Olive oil spray

Instructions

1. Preheat the oven to 180°C.

2. Boil the butternut until tender, then cut into small cubes.

3. Place phyllo pastry layers into muffin moulds or ramekins, lightly spraying with olive oil for crispiness. Bake for 10 minutes until golden.

4. In a pan, roast the cubed butternut with honey, cinnamon, salt, and pepper.

5. Fill the phyllo cups with cream cheese mixed with chives, then top with the roasted butternut cubes.

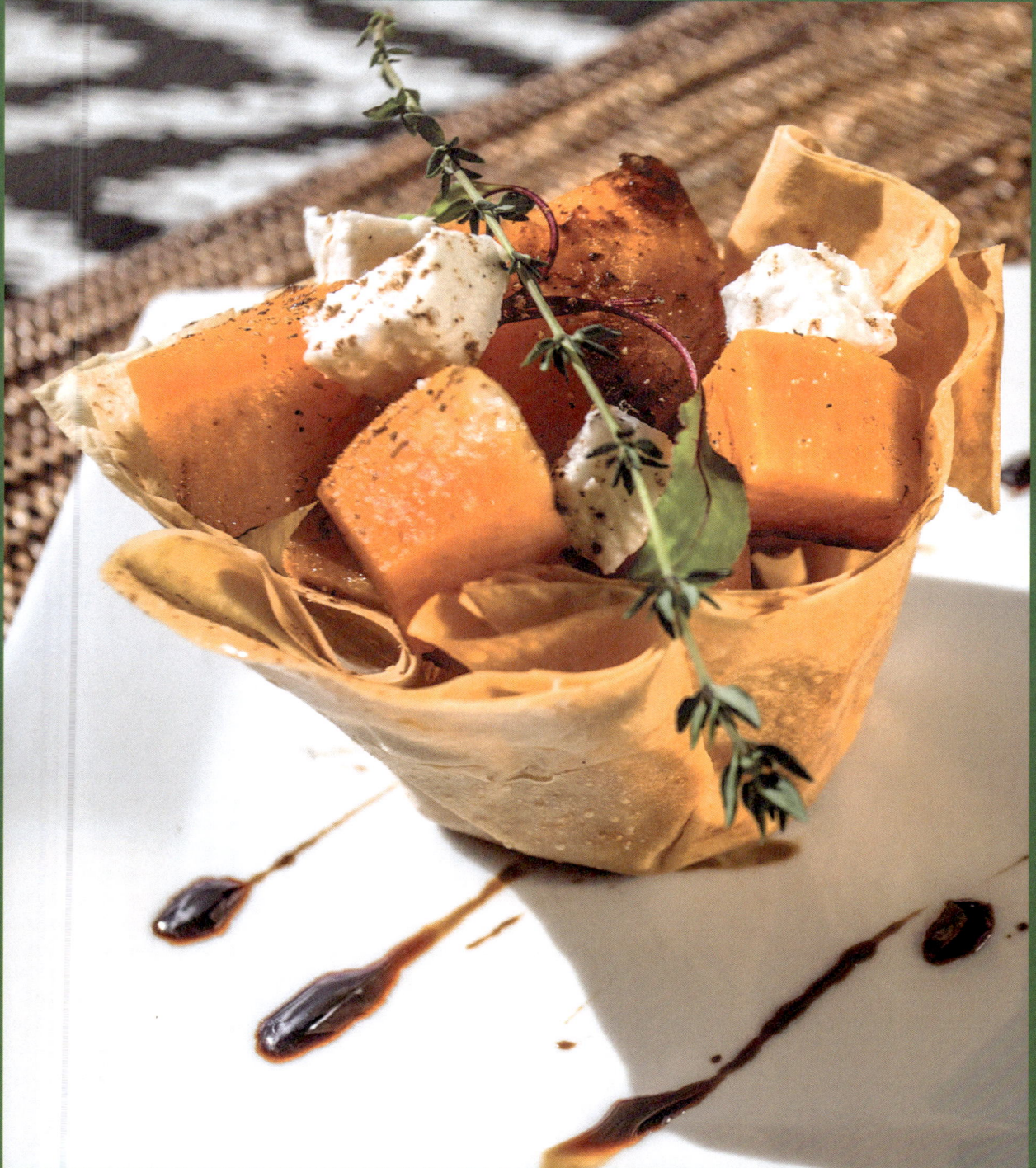

Sweet Potato Gratin Dauphinois

serves 2 (main)
serves 4 (side)

Ingredients

450g sweet potato
½ tsp cinnamon
¼ tsp cumin
⅛ tsp cayenne pepper
½ tsp turmeric
3 garlic cloves, grated
1 tbsp olive oil
250ml milk
250ml heavy cream
50g parmesan, grated
Small knob of butter
Fine sea salt

Instructions

1. Preheat the oven to 200°C.

2. Peel the sweet potato and slice them thinly using a mandoline. Place in a bowl.

3. Mix cinnamon, cumin, cayenne, turmeric, grated garlic, and olive oil. Rub the sweet potato slices with the mixture.

4. Combine milk, cream, and a pinch of salt.

5. Assemble the gratin: Butter a casserole dish. Pour in ⅓ of the milk-cream mixture, then arrange half the potato slices. Sprinkle with half the parmesan. Add another ⅓ of the milk-cream mixture, then the remaining potato slices. Pour in the remaining milk-cream mixture and press the potatoes gently so the liquid surrounds them. Sprinkle with the remaining parmesan.

6. Bake in the oven for 40-50 minutes until the sweet potatoes are tender. If the top browns too quickly, cover loosely with foil.

7. Remove from the oven and let rest for 5-10 minutes before serving.

Always believe something wonderful is about to happen.

Desserts

Coffee and coconut cheesecake

Coffee and chocolate tart

Caramelised pear and chocolate cheesecake

Amarula crème brûlée

Tarte Tatin

Crème caramel

Sublime dark chocolate tart with orange coulis

Chantilly granadilla cheesecake with red berry coulis

Nougat glacé and red berry coulis

Cappuccino ice cream

Strawberries and banana sugar-free ice cream

Fresh fruit sorbet

Vegan banana ice cream

Coffee and Coconut Cheesecake

serves 8

Ingredients

1 packet Tennis or digestive biscuits

50g melted butter

360g condensed milk (1 tin)

280g cream cheese

3 tbsp coconut powder

2 tbsp (good) instant coffee

100ml hot water

Instructions

1. Preheat the oven to 150°C.

2. Crush the biscuits and mix with melted butter. Press firmly into a tart dish to form a compact base.

3. Mix condensed milk, cream cheese, and coconut powder until smooth.

4. Dissolve the instant coffee in 100ml of hot water and mix into the filling.

5. Pour the filling over the biscuit base and bake in the oven for 30-40 minutes until set.

6. Allow to cool before serving.

A recipe created by mistake. Making a simple cheesecake, I asked my staff for lemons to help regulate the sweetness of the condensed milk. When I realised there were no lemons in view, apart from those in a shop 50km away, I had to make a plan. I grabbed the coffee and some coconut powder and added them to the mixture. This coffee cheesecake became one of the most popular desserts at our safari lodge and tented camp.

One of the most popular desserts at our lodge.

Coffee and Chocolate Tart

serves 8

Ingredients

for the base

1 packet Tennis or digestive biscuits

Melted butter (enough to make the base compact)

for the filling

1 tin condensed milk

1 pot crème fraîche

1 cup liquid cream

3 egg yolks

3 tsp (good) instant coffee dissolved in a little hot water

for the topping

70g dark chocolate

½ cup liquid cream

Instructions

1. Preheat the oven to 140°C.

2. Crush the biscuits and mix with melted butter. Press firmly into the bottom of a tart dish to form a compact base.

3. Mix the condensed milk, crème fraîche, dissolved coffee, and egg yolks until smooth. Pour over the biscuit base.

4. Bake for 20 minutes in the oven. Switch off the oven and let the tart settle for 10 minutes.

5. Melt the chocolate with the liquid cream until smooth.

6. Once cooled in the fridge, pour the chocolate-cream mixture over the tart.

7. Cool for 1 hour before serving.

Tip: Slow, low-temperature baking is the secret to the tart's smooth, luscious texture.

Caramelised Pear and Chocolate Cheesecake

serves 8

Ingredients

for the base

1 packet Tennis biscuits (200g)

Melted butter (enough to press biscuits compactly into tart dish)

for the filling

1 tin condensed milk (365g)

1 pot cream cheese (250g)

6 fresh pears

20g butter (for caramelising)

1 tbsp vanilla essence

for the topping

70g dark chocolate

½ cup liquid cream

Instructions

1. Preheat the oven to 140°C.
2. Crush the biscuits, mix with melted butter, and press firmly into the bottom of a tart dish.
3. In a pan, add sugar and melt until caramel forms. Add the butter to stop it from solidifying. Cook the pears for 3 minutes, turning until slightly softened.
4. Mix condensed milk with cream cheese and vanilla essence.
5. Place the caramelised pears over the biscuit base and pour the creamy mixture on top.
6. Cook in the oven for 30-40 minutes.
7. Allow the tart to cool for a couple of hours.
8. Prepare chocolate sauce: Melt chocolate with liquid cream over very low heat, stirring continuously.
9. Pour the chocolate sauce over the cooled cheesecake. Chill for a further couple of hours before serving.

Amarula Crème Brûlée

serves 8

Ingredients

1 litre liquid cream

10 egg yolks

150g sugar

1 vanilla bean (or 2 tsp vanilla essence)

200ml Amarula

Sugar, for caramelising the top

Instructions

1. In a pot, gently heat the cream. Split the vanilla bean, scrape the seeds into the cream, and add the pod to infuse. Do not boil. Once warm, remove from the stove and allow to marinate.

2. Separate the eggs and place the yolks in a large bowl. Mix with sugar until smooth and pale. That is important. The smoother, the better.

3. Slowly pour the warm cream into the egg yolks, stirring constantly. Remove the vanilla pod.

4. Pour the mixture into individual ramekins.

5. Place the ramekins in a water bath in the oven at 120°C. Cooking time depends on the size: small square dishes ~25 minutes, large ramekins ~35 minutes.

6. Remove when set. It should be slightly wobbly in the centre.

7. Allow to cool, then refrigerate for a few hours.

8. Make caramel and pour it in a lacy pattern on baking paper. Once hardened, place on top of the chilled crème brûlée before serving. Alternatively, sprinkle or pour caramel directly onto the cold custard.

Tarte Tatin

serves 1

Ingredients

1 apple

50g sugar (for caramel)

Puff pastry (enough for one tart)

A pinch of cinnamon

Butter (a small knob, optional, to stop caramel cooking)

1 individual tart dish

Instructions

1. In a small pan, heat the sugar until it caramelises. Add a small knob of butter to stop cooking if desired. Pour half of the caramel into the tart dish.

2. Cut the apple in half and place the rounded side down in the centre of the dish. Arrange the remaining quarters around it.

3. Pour the rest of the caramel over the apples and sprinkle with a pinch of cinnamon.

4. Place the tart dish in the oven at 180°C for 15 minutes.

5. Cut a circle of puff pastry to fit the tart dish. Place it over the apples.

6. Return the tart to the oven and bake for 30 minutes, until the pastry is golden and cooked through.

7. To serve, turn the tart upside down so the pastry ends up at the bottom. Serve warm or cold with ice cream or whipped cream.

This delicious dessert has an interesting story. It was created by accident in the late 1800s by Stephanie Tatin. She simply forgot to put the pastry at the bottom of the tart dish. When she realised her mistake, she decided to put the pastry on top; then, after baking, she simply turned it around so that the pastry would be at the bottom. The result was an incredible hit with the guests of her Paris restaurant. Thus was born the tarte Tatin, one of the most classic desserts in French cuisine.

One of the most classic desserts in French cuisine.

Crème Caramel

serves 8

Ingredients

1 litre milk

6 eggs

100g sugar (divided)

1 vanilla pod or 2 tsp vanilla essence

8 ramekins

Instructions

1. Preheat the oven to 150°C.

2. Heat 60g of sugar in a pan over a high heat until it turns golden brown. Pour immediately into 8 individual ramekins to coat the base.

3. Boil the milk with a split vanilla pod or add vanilla essence. Let it cool slightly.

4. Whisk the eggs with the remaining sugar until smooth. Gradually, pour in the lukewarm milk in a thin stream, stirring constantly.

5. Pour the mixture into the caramel-lined ramekins. Place the ramekins in a bain-marie and bake for 45 minutes.

6. Allow to cool, then store in the fridge.

7. To serve, invert the ramekin onto a plate and optionally serve with a scoop of ice cream.

A winner is a loser who tried one more time.

The chocolate and chilli tart experiment

It was a great idea, but too much chilli put my game ranger, Brendan, into shock some 25 years ago, when he took a piece of it at 6am before taking guests on a game drive. He told me he was hungry and it was the only food he could find in the fridge that morning.

The chocolate and chilli tart experiment clearly landed in the 'dangerously creative' category. But hey, every masterpiece needs a few brave tasters along the way... even if they didn't volunteer!

This tart must have been one of the eight experimental chocolate tarts I had to create before achieving perfection with our sublime chocolate tart, now one of our signature desserts.

We called it SUBLIME, because why be modest when you create the best?

Sublime Dark Chocolate Tart
with Orange Coulis

serves 1

Ingredients

200g 70% dark chocolate
1 pot crème fraîche (250g)
1½ tbsp condensed milk
½ cup liquid cream
3 egg yolks
1 packet Tennis or digestive biscuits
30g butter

for the orange coulis

Juice of 2 oranges
½ tsp cornflour (Maizena)

Instructions

Prepare the chocolate filling

1. Melt the dark chocolate in a bain-marie.
2. Beat the egg yolks.
3. Once the chocolate has cooled slightly, fold the egg yolks slowly into the chocolate.
4. Mix the liquid cream and crème fraîche together, then combine with the chocolate mixture.

Prepare the tart base

1. Crush the biscuits and mix with the melted butter to form a smooth paste.
2. Line the bottom of the tart dish with baking paper.
3. Press the biscuit mixture into the bottom to create a compact base.
4. Pour the chocolate mixture over the base.

Cooking

1. Bake at a very low temperature (130°C) for 25 minutes.
2. Switch off the oven and leave the tart inside for another 20 minutes to set gently.
3. Chill in the fridge or cooler room for at least 3 hours.

Prepare the orange coulis

1. Heat the orange juice with cornflour (Maizena) until smooth.
2. Serve over the tart (optional: can also be made with strawberry coulis).

*Failure is success
in progress.*

Albert Einstein

The camembert and roquefort ice-cream disaster

Among my more… creative culinary experiments, one truly deserves a place in the 'what was I thinking' hall of fame – Camembert and Roquefort ice-cream with raspberry coulis.

Yes, really.

I wasn't quite sure whether it was meant to be a starter or a dessert, so I did what any wildly overconfident kitchen dreamer might do – I tested it directly on my unsuspecting lunch guests. Proudly, I presented the dish myself, expecting nods of approval, raised eyebrows of delight, and maybe even a few gasps of admiration. I'd dared to blend the boldness of French cheese with the sweetness of berries. Surely, this was brilliance?

Well, what I received were the kind of comments that sound like compliments but aren't.

"Interesting."

"Very creative."

"Never had that before!"

Out of ten guests, only one claimed to enjoy it – and she was French. To this day, I'm not sure whether she was being polite, patriotic, or just felt sorry for me and my melting disaster of a dish.

Needless to say, the Camembert and Roquefort ice-cream never made it back onto the menu. Ever. Though in my defence, at least I dared to try.

Even failed haute cuisine has its place in the storybook of Thula Thula.

Chantilly Granadilla Cheesecake
with Red Berry Coulis

serves 4

Ingredients

125g cream cheese (½ cup)

150ml liquid cream (½ cup, to whip)

Pulp of 3 granadillas (or 1 small tin)

½ packet Tennis or digestive biscuits

20g melted butter

30g melted dark chocolate

Fresh berries, to garnish

50g frozen berries, plus 1 tsp honey and juice of ½ lemon (for coulis)

7cm high circle mould (without bottom)

Instructions

1. Mix the cream cheese with the granadilla pulp.
2. Whip the cream until firm, then fold gently into the cream cheese and passion fruit mixture.
3. Prepare the base by crushing the biscuits and mixing with the melted butter. Press at the bottom of the circle mould.
4. Pour the melted chocolate over the biscuit base.
5. Add the cream and passion fruit mixture on top of the chocolate layer.
6. Pour some red berry coulis over and around the cheesecake.
7. Garnish with fresh berries and a few mint leaves.

Red berry coulis

1. Blend 50g frozen berries with honey and lemon juice in a food processor until smooth.
2. Chill for at least 2-3 hours before serving.

If you want to make everyone happy, don't be a leader.

Sell ice-cream.

Steve Jobs

All our ice-creams are homemade. The main reason is that in South Africa, where we are based anyway, you cannot find such a selection of flavours in any shop.

So, we created them in the kitchen of the Elephant Safari Lodge, with fresh ingredients, savoir-faire, and love.

Nougat Glacé and Red Berry Coulis

serves 8

Ingredients

200g sugar
100ml honey
200g blanched almonds
8 egg whites
100ml liquid fresh cream
4 sheets phyllo pastry (30 x 30cm)
Fresh or frozen red berries
Juice of 1 lemon

Instructions

Nougat glacé

1. Heat the sugar slowly in a non-stick pan until it turns light brown.
2. Add the honey and almonds, mixing carefully. Transfer onto baking paper to cool.
3. Whip the egg whites until firm.
4. Chill and whip the cream until firm.
5. Break the nougat into small pieces.
6. Gently fold the nougat into the egg whites and whipped cream mixture.
7. Transfer into a terrine dish and freeze for 12 hours.

Red berry coulis

1. Blend the berries with lemon juice until smooth.
2. Chill in the fridge until serving.

Phyllo pastry rounds

1. Preheat the oven to 160°C.
2. Using a 7cm round cutter, cut 32 rounds from the phyllo sheets.
3. Brush each round with butter and bake at 180°C for about 10 minutes, until lightly golden. Cool in a dry place.

To serve

1. Place 2 rounds of phyllo pastry on each plate.
2. Use a round mould to pour the nougat glacé onto the phyllo base.
3. Cover with 2 more phyllo rounds.
4. Top with fresh berries. Drizzle the coulis on top of and around the nougat. Garnish with mint and icing sugar.

Cappuccino Ice-Cream

serves 6

Ingredients

320ml fresh liquid cream

45g freshly ground coffee (Jamaica blend)

4 egg yolks

150g caster sugar

320ml whipped cream

Instructions

1. Heat the fresh cream slowly until just below boiling.

2. Add the ground coffee, stir well, and allow to infuse for 30 minutes.

3. In a bowl, whisk the egg yolks and sugar until thick and pale.

4. Reheat the coffee-infused cream until almost boiling.

5. Strain the cream through a sieve. Pour it slowly onto the egg yolk mixture, stirring constantly.

6. Cool the mixture for 1 hour.

7. Whip the cream until firm.

8. Gently fold the whipped cream into the coffee and egg mixture.

9. Pour into a terrine mould and freeze for at least 6 hours.

10. Serve in scoops. Drizzle with fine, melted dark chocolate. Add extra whipped cream on the side.

Strawberries and Banana Sugar-Free Ice-Cream

serves 4

Ingredients

2 frozen bananas

2 cups frozen strawberries

1 pot of crème fraîche (or a tin of coconut cream for a vegan version)

1 tsp vanilla essence

2 tbsp Xylitol (or preferred sugar substitute)

Instructions

1. Slice the bananas into coins and place them in a sealable bag in the freezer until solid.

2. Combine the frozen bananas, strawberries, crème fraîche (or coconut cream), vanilla, and Xylitol in a food processor or blender. Process until smooth.

3. Pour the mixture into a container and freeze until firm.

Fresh Fruit Sorbet

serves 8

Ingredients

for the sorbet syrup
600ml water
400g caster sugar

Instructions

for the sorbet syrup
1. Combine the water and caster sugar in a pot.
2. Bring to a boil, stirring to dissolve the sugar.
3. Set aside to cool.

This will yield about 1 litre of sorbet syrup, ready to mix with the puréed fruit of your choice.

preparation of the sorbet
1. Purée or mash your chosen fruit until smooth.
2. Stir in the cooled syrup, using the suggested fruit-to-syrup ratios below.
3. Pour the mixture into a container and freeze for at least 12 hours, or until firm.

suggested fruit-to-syrup ratios
1 pineapple → 100ml syrup
2 mangoes → 100ml syrup
1 packet frozen red berries → 200ml syrup
1 pawpaw → 100ml syrup
4 kiwis → 200ml syrup

Vegan Banana Ice-Cream

serves 4-6

Ingredients

4 medium ripe bananas

300ml full-fat coconut milk

55g caster sugar

A few tbsp of crushed nuts (optional)

Instructions

1. Peel the bananas and place them in a blender. Blend until smooth.

2. Add the coconut milk and caster sugar. Whisk together for a few minutes until fully combined.

3. Gently fold in any mix-ins, such as crushed nuts, if using.

4. Transfer the mixture to a freezer-proof dish with a lid and freeze for 2 hours.

5. Remove from the freezer and whisk again for a few minutes to smooth out any frozen lumps.

6. Return to the freezer for a further 8-10 hours, whisking every few hours to prevent ice crystals from forming.

7. Before serving, allow the ice cream to sit at room temperature for a few minutes to soften slightly. Scoop into cones or bowls and enjoy!

Romantic champagne picnic in the bush

Our romantic bush picnics are always a highlight for our guests. The game rangers scout out the perfect scenic spot within the reserve – an open view, vast skies, and the sounds of nature – and our chefs prepare a light, gourmet lunch. The setting is straight from *Out of Africa* – a beautifully laid table, linen napkins, sparkling glasses of champagne, and nothing but the wild around you. Peaceful. Serene.

Until Thabo and Ntombi decide to crash the party.

In the early days, our two beloved rhinos were still a little too humanised. Curious, affectionate, and utterly unbothered by social etiquette, they would wander over to the picnic setup, drawn by the sound of laughter (or perhaps the smell of interesting new creations).

But knowing Thabo's occasionally unpredictable behaviour – and to avoid asking guests to climb the nearest tree for safety – we eventually fenced off the picnic area with a single electrified wire. Just one line, discreetly placed. Still, 8,000 volts sends a message of NO ENTRY to two-tonne gate crashers.

Champagne picnic lunch
in the bush

Thabo and Ntombi would still come. They would stand behind the wire, watching intently as guests sipped champagne and nibbled on canapés. Two sad, soulful faces peering through the bush, as if asking why they had been left off the guest list. Especially Thabo. He had perfected the art of sad puppy eyes, a master of emotional manipulation in rhino form.

Those were the days when Thabo and Ntombi were still a bit too 'humanised' or 'habituated' to humans. But it also reminded us of the bittersweet transition these orphans had to make to become truly wild rhinos.

Today, with the expansion of Thula Thula to over 5,000 hectares, Thabo and Ntombi roam freely through the reserve.

They are no longer seeking human company; they have found their place among their own kind. They are monitored 24/7 by our anti-poaching team and game rangers for their protection, but no more fences – or picnic invitations – are needed.

They are wild now, as they were always meant to be. And we, their human family, still watch over them.

Always.

The wedding, the curry, and the elephant

Weddings are always a special occasion – joyful, heartfelt ceremonies that we prepare for with great care. Every detail matters. The flowers, the music, the atmosphere. But for me, one of the most important elements is the food.

I've always believed that a wedding menu should be personal. Something created with love, something that reflects the couple and, if possible, their cultural roots. I try to tailor the menu to the guests' countries of origin, blending a bit of French creativity with a dash of African flavour. Or sometimes the other way around.

This wedding was particularly close to my heart. It was my dear friend Iva's big day – her third time walking down the aisle – and she had chosen Thula Thula as the setting for her celebration. I wanted everything to be perfect. But more than perfect, I wanted it to be unforgettable.

And unforgettable, it was.

In an ambitious burst of creativity, I decided to serve a crocodile curry vol-au-vent, topped with a chocolate and chilli sauce. A bold experiment, and one that I hoped would dazzle.

It didn't.

The Master of Ceremonies described the dish as 'memorable'. I don't think it was a compliment. But, as he put it, it was 'something they'd never had before and would remember for the rest of their lives'. Thankfully, the cake was a resounding success – a stunning creation by my pastry chef, Fortunate. At least we ended the meal on a high note.

As the sun began to dip and the celebration moved into the evening, the Zulu dancers took their place in front of the lodge veranda to perform for the newlyweds. Drums beat, feet stomped, and the air filled with the rhythm of a thousand-year-old warrior dance.

And then Numzane arrived.

Our massive bull elephant appeared quietly behind the perimeter fence. Towering, calm, and curious – perhaps drawn by the music, or maybe just wanting to join the festivities. The dancers froze. The guests, wide-eyed, slowly began to back away.

We had no choice but to move the entire wedding party to the other side of the lodge. But Numzane, determined and rather intrigued, simply circled the fence and followed us. The fencing around the lodge carries 10,000 volts — a deterrent, not a guarantee. If an elephant really wants to come through, he will.

The Zulu dancers, brave as they were, looked visibly shaken. So were we.

In the end, we returned to the front veranda, hoping that Numzane might take the hint. He did. Feeling unwelcome with all these humans who keep running away from him, he slowly turned and walked away.

Our spectacular wedding cakes

He wasn't being aggressive. Just lonely. A solitary bull looking for connection.

It brought back a wave of emotion. I remembered the day he arrived at Thula Thula, a young orphan whose mother had been killed. I remembered his early days in the boma, isolated, bullied by the others, mostly by Nana and Frankie. Always an outsider. Never fully part of the herd.

Numzane had a difficult beginning. A tragic one. And yet, he became a legend. Unforgettable, not just for his size and presence, but for the silent story he carried.

His moment at the wedding – unexpected, a little chaotic, and entirely real – reminded me once again that nature doesn't follow scripts. And that the greatest lessons at Thula Thula have always come from the animals themselves.

In the end, it wasn't the crocodile curry, the towering cake, or even the dance that made Iva's wedding unforgettable.

It was Numzane. And it was love – in all its forms.

Cooking classes at the
Elephant Safari Lodge

Head Chef, Tom
(the baby elephant rescuer)

The memorable champagne breakfast

South African wines are outstanding.

Since arriving in 1987, I've witnessed the extraordinary growth and evolution of the South African wine industry. It's a spectacular success story, and I'm proud to serve only South African wines and Méthode Champenoise sparkling wines at our safari lodge, the tented camp, and the Volunteers Academy. But not everyone shares my enthusiasm.

One evening, many moons ago, when we had just opened the safari lodge, Mabona called me, clearly in a mild state of panic. "We have guests," she said, "demanding only French Champagne and French wine." When I met them, I understood why she was stressed. 'Demanding' was actually a bit of an understatement.

I tied to explain, very politely, that we served some of the best South African 'champagnes'. In fact, in a blind tasting, I told them that even as a French person, I wouldn't be able to tell the difference. I wanted to praise South African winemaking talent and stand up for the local brilliance.

One lady looked at me with a slight air of disdain and said, "Well, your palate is different from our palate."

Ah. OK, then.

They were all South Africans themselves, who had apparently already enjoyed a few beers and several spirits, so let's just say their palates had been through a bit of a workout by then. But anyway – the client is king, or in this case, a very particular queen. I promised her French Champagne for breakfast. They smiled, relaxed, and enjoyed a fabulous dinner. No one was threatening to leave anymore or have me fired. Ha, ha, funny. I would have had to fire myself.

The next morning, I sent one of our rangers on an emergency mission to Empangeni to fetch a case of French Champagne from the local bottle store. I suspected that this luxury item wasn't exactly flying off the shelves in Zululand. Indeed, our loyal ranger returned triumphantly with six bottles.

By the time our guests returned from their morning game drive, the Champagne was perfectly chilled and waiting at their breakfast table.

I watched discreetly as the first bottle was opened. As per etiquette, no tasting – Champagne is simply poured. But when I saw the colour of the liquid, my heart sank. A darkish yellow. Definitely not normal. And then I noticed there were no bubbles.

A bubbly without bubbles. Funny, hey?

The Champagne had clearly aged, and not gracefully. I imagine it had been sitting for too many years in some dark corner of that shop. But our guests loved it. Phew!

By the third bottle, they were positively glowing. Laughing, clinking glasses, praising the 'exquisite taste' of this French delicacy. I was so relieved that they didn't offer me a glass. Because my palate, French or not, would have flatly rejected it.

Those were the days…

To all our special guests

The early years at Thula Thula were marked by humble beginnings and more than a few tough moments – times we will never forget. It was an interesting learning curve, to say the least.

Today, we count ourselves incredibly lucky to welcome the most wonderful guests. Many of you have read our books, followed our journey, and truly understood who we are and what we stand for.

You come not just for a safari, but for the love, passion, and vision for nature and wildlife conservation that radiates through everyone at Thula Thula.

Thank you – to all of you special humans.

You are, and always will be, part of the Thula Thula family.

Welcome to the luxury tented camp

Creation of the luxury Tented Camp (2006)

Pleasing everyone is never easy, but we still tried.

After six years at the *Elephant Safari Lodge*, and after countless conversations with guests, I realised there was a growing need for an alternative. Something closer to nature, and more suitable for families with young children. The lodge, while beautiful, wasn't really designed with them in mind.

This kind of informal 'market research', gathered simply by listening to guest feedback and observing their preferences, made it clear – we needed to offer something different. A more relaxed, family-friendly experience. Something simpler, more connected to nature – a contrast to the manicured lawns and refined cuisine of the main lodge.

And so, the idea of a luxury tented camp was born.

While offering the full comfort of a four-star lodge, the camp brought guests closer to the bush. The tents gave a more authentic nature experience, and the food matched the atmosphere – simple, generous, and familiar. Home-style meals served buffet-style – hearty, comforting, and unpretentious.

And it worked like a dream.

I won't go into detail about the recipes as they were straightforward – the classic South African braai (barbecue), potjie (stew), roast chicken, and roast beef. The kind of food you'd expect at a Sunday lunch with family. Except it happened every day, and everyone loved it.

Memorable New Year's Eve at our freshly opened Tented Camp

When you are a city girl like me, we are used to water just coming out of the tap. When you live in the bush, with elephants, it is not always true. Water is essential, for humans and animals alike, and we would not survive without it. And we certainly would not be able to cook. As simple as that.

That New Year's Eve was a special one. We prepared a five-course feast for our resident guests at our newly-built luxury tented camp. We had opened a week before and had welcomed our very first guests.

Then, water from the tap just stopped, but ironically, that evening, it was pouring with rain. We still had hope as dinner was a couple of hours away. We started looking for the cause of this water shortage. Suddenly, a doubt came to my mind. Elephants love clean water, not the muddy water that flows when it is raining.

I came out of the main area and I could feel their presence. Elephants, with their huge mass, can move around so silently, but you can smell them, sense them.

Somehow, you just know they are around.

Getting closer in the heavy rain, I could see them, all of them, taking turns to drink from the water pipe, the clean water they are so fond of. Such bliss to watch them enjoying that moment!

But I also knew we were doomed for the whole night. No one can approach a herd of elephants and ask them to stop drinking and kindly move away so that we can fix the broken pipe.

We had a similar situation when they invaded my fruit and vegetable garden years ago.

At least they provided great entertainment for our guests that evening and we happily celebrated the New Year, offering champagne to all as an apology to the naughty behaviour of our babas. We used all of the available mineral water for cooking, while our muddy guests used it for washing until the following morning when the elephants decided to move on. Looking for more delicious clean water at the Safari Lodge maybe?

We decided to address this challenging situation. We just buried our water pipes a bit deeper in the ground.

As simple as that!

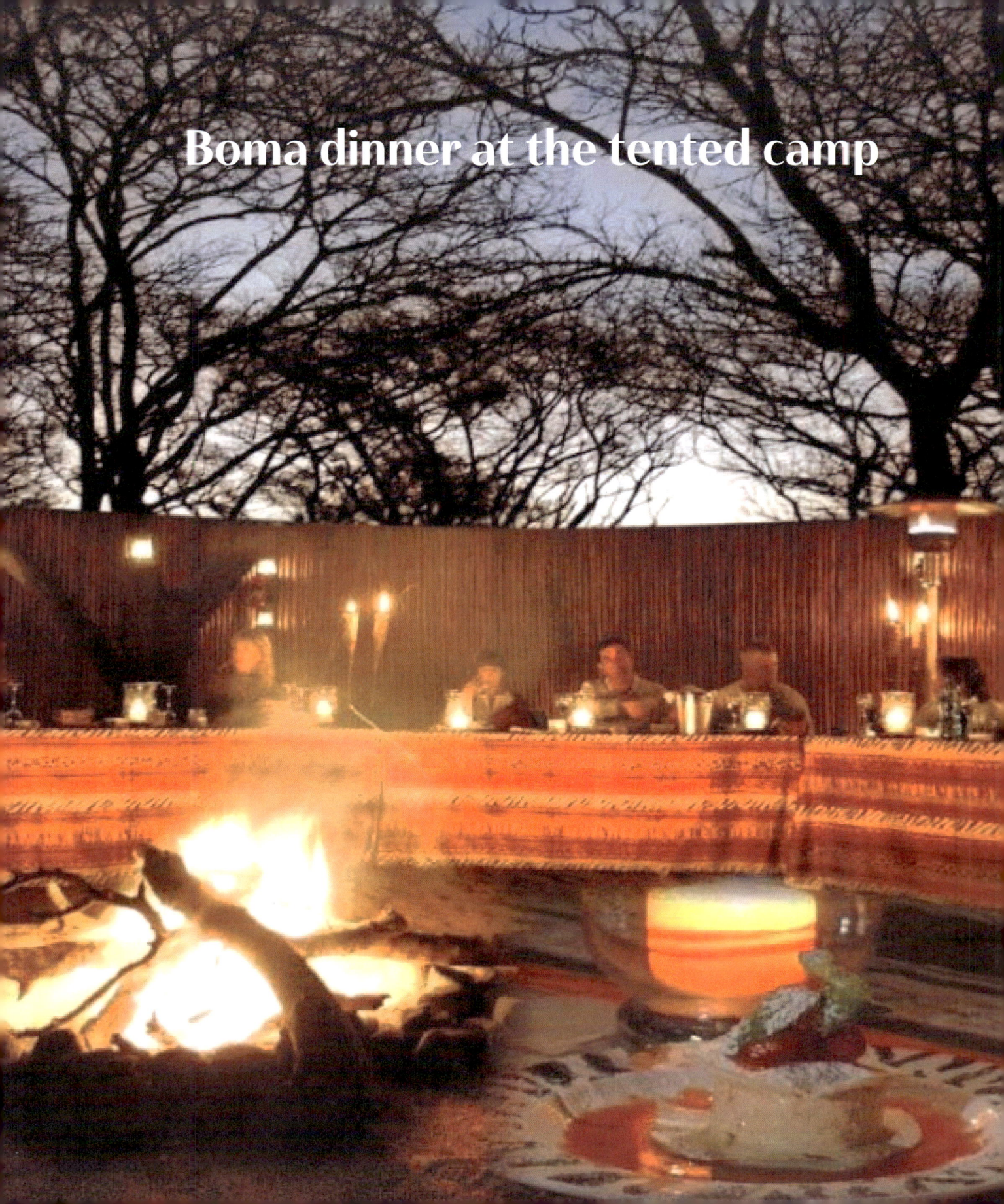

Boma dinner at the tented camp

When Thabo and Ntombi raided the Boma

Thabo and Ntombi, our beloved orphan rhinos, were released into the wild at 18 months old, but never without the watchful eyes of their dedicated carer and a security guard For their safety, of course.

One evening, I was hosting dinner in the boma, our open-air dining area at the tented camp when two massive, silent shapes appeared out of the darkness. Up the two steps they climbed, calm and confident, like they owned the place. And in a way, they did.

Their carer and security guard were right behind them, frantically trying to steer them back towards the garden, but Thabo and Ntombi had already decided that dinner with the guests sounded far more entertaining than grazing under the stars. You can't really argue with a couple of two-ton rhinos.

We just had time to whisper a hasty warning to our guests: Grab your plates and your glasses, and quietly move inside. A mild panic (mixed with a lot of laughter) swept through the boma as everyone fled to the indoor dining area, hoping our oversized party crashers wouldn't follow.

Once the dust settled, we tiptoed back to assess the damage only to find them both peacefully napping in the middle of the boma, blissfully unaware of the evening's chaos.

Just another night with Thabo and Ntombi, the adorable dinner crashers of Thula Thula.

Happy happy monkeys

One day at the tented camp, we noticed some very odd behaviour from our resident troop of monkeys. They weren't just being their usual mischievous selves. They were unusually joyful, jumping around with what looked like a bit too much excitement, even for monkeys.

As it turned out, they had managed to sneak into a guest tent that hadn't been properly closed. Inside, they discovered a treasure trove – a pack of jelly beans.

Not just any jelly beans. These were infused with THC – that's marijuana, for those not up to date with California's latest legal snacks. Brought in, of course, by our well-meaning guests from the US.

The monkeys were ecstatic. That day, for once, they showed zero interest in stealing food from the lunch buffet. Just a troop of stoned, content little primates, giggling in the trees (or at least, that's how it looked to us).

Let's just say that the happy pills did the job.

There's an elephant at the bar

The strangest message from the hostess at the tented camp crackled over the radio: "There is an elephant at the bar."

A moment of panic. Everyone froze. Then, chaos. Staff rushed to the scene. We all know that elephants are NOT allowed at the bar.

It was early morning, just before the game drives. Guests were slowly gathering in the lounge, half-awake, easing into the day with coffee, tea, and rusks. A peaceful bush morning – until this unexpected guest made an entrance.

As it turned out, the elephant in question was Mabula, our special big bull. And no, he wasn't exactly at the bar. He had, rather quietly, made his way to the swimming pool.

Mabula, it seems, was simply thirsty and fancied a morning drink from the clear blue pool. That is all. He stood there, completely unfazed, gazing at the humans who had emerged from their tents, coffee cups in hand, to find a massive elephant quietly hydrating just metres away.

Quite the wake-up call.

The game rangers quickly stepped in, gently guiding guests away from our 'big baba', reminding them that while Mabula may look calm, he could be unpredictable. He was Frankie's son, our previous strong-willed matriarch, and the late mischievous Numzane's best friend. He had learnt from the best how to gatecrash and create panic mode around humans.

Off everyone went on their game drive, a little more awake than usual. They carried with them the rare and unforgettable memory of sipping coffee next to an elephant at the pool.

Just another morning in the wilds of Thula Thula.

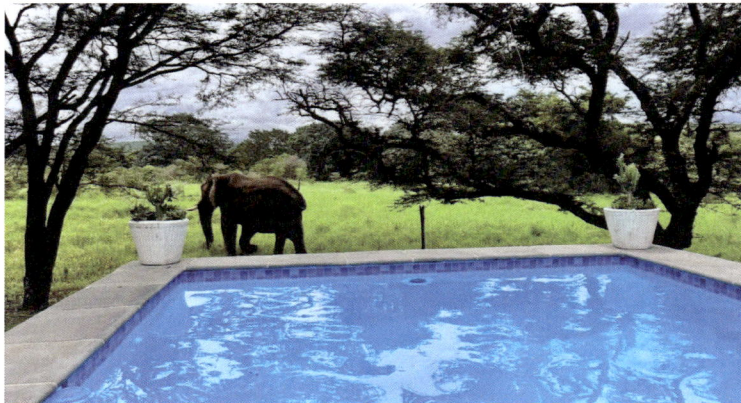

Great things in business are never done by one person, they're done by a team of people.

The Tented Camp team

A soulful journey with purpose

To my team, the beating heart of Thula Thula, your loyalty, skill, humour, and endless patience have been my greatest joy. You met every challenge with grace, every animal encounter with calm, and prepared every dish with love. Witnessing your progress and transformation over the years has brought me immense joy and a profound sense of accomplishment.

Thank you for giving this place its soul.

And of course, it is a story of the animals. They were not just visitors, but our unspoken teachers. From the quiet wisdom of the elephants, to the sharp-eyed confidence of the cheetah, the mischief of the monkeys, and the cheeky visits of night creatures like the bush baby, we learnt what it means to coexist. They reminded us, daily, that we are guests here. That the wilderness is not ours to own, but to honour and protect.

Every guest was a thread in the great tapestry of connection between people and nature. And every wildlife sighting was a reminder of why we must continue to protect what remains.

As we close this chapter and step into new ones, I carry with me immense gratitude – for the journey, for the challenges that shaped us, for the privilege of serving food surrounded by the wild, and for every guest who sat at our table and left with a piece of Africa in their heart.

The *Elephant Safari Lodge* team

"
Helping others to build a future for themselves is what will determine the significance of our own journey.

It is all about making a difference to the lives of others.
"